An Irregular
Girlhood in Hitler's
Shadow

An Irregular Girlhood in Hitler's Shadow

✦

A Memoir

Vera Haldy-Regier

iUniverse, Inc.
New York Lincoln Shanghai

An Irregular Girlhood in Hitler's Shadow
A Memoir

iUniverse books may be ordered through booksellers or by contacting:

iUniverse
2021 Pine Lake Road, Suite 100
Lincoln, NE 68512
www.iuniverse.com
1-800-Authors (1-800-288-4677)

ISBN-13: 978-0-595-38652-9 (pbk)
ISBN-13: 978-0-595-83033-6 (ebk)
ISBN-10: 0-595-38652-0 (pbk)
ISBN-10: 0-595-83033-1 (ebk)

Printed in the United States of America

In memory of my mother, Nora,
And for the countless other displaced wanderers
In search of new beginnings.

Cranes in migration,
wings beating at the wind,
necks stretching forward
with passionate purpose
in search of welcoming meadows.
By the thousands
we have joined their journey,
the anguished beating of our hearts:
a drum song
announcing our hopes
for a new home
before the first snow.

—Vera Haldy-Regier

Contents

List of Illustrations

Preface

My family and I spent the entire Second World War in Tsingtao, China, a German outpost that received a 99-year lease for that port as a concessionary "plum" of the Opium War that Britain won in 1842. The lease was enacted much later, in 1896, and was signed that year by Prince Heinrich, brother of Kaiser Wilhelm. Many concessions were asked of the Chinese and the victory benefited Britain, France, Germany and Russia with lucrative trade agreements. Germany was no exception in profiting and establishing its Pacific fleet presence in the strategic port of Tsingtao on the Yellow Sea in Shandong Province.

The Boxer Rebellion, begun in 1901 by the Manchu Dowager in order to free China of the rampant foreign imperialism, was quashed and foreign influences continued to reign in China. Britain held sway over Hong Kong; France over Viet Nam and Portugal over Macao. All the major European powers carved up Shanghai and established a legendary, colorful high life in that city that flourished throughout the Second World War except for the refugees from Europe and Russia who largely lived in enforced, ghetto-squalor.

Until 1914, Tsingtao was the capital city of Germany's Chinese lease territory, which included the surrounding area on the Shandong Peninsula. Then, in 1914, the Japanese took over the area, subsequently giving it back to the Chinese until 1938, when the Japanese regained it once again. That made for a cozy relationship during World War II between the Germans and Japanese.

So, as early as the turn of the century, Germans, lived and traded there, built factories, started businesses and flourished in a culture very foreign to them but on which they left their marked imprint. They built neat little villas with red tiled roofs, imported German goods for their consumption, brewed fine beer and exported Chinese goods to Europe.

When Hitler ascended to power, Tsingtao could not escape his attention. Nor did Naples or Istanbul where my parents lived before Tsingtao. Any place with a German consulate and a German community was a potential target for conversion to Nazism. What's more, Hitler was a keen strategist and knew how best to extend his long, and mighty arm: He planted his most fervent followers in the midst of distant, untainted communities and charged them with the task of converting the "heathen". Or he sent "recalcitrant" Germans such as my father to toe the line under the zealous Nazi "Group Leaders," as they were called.

As a matter of fact, his strategy might today be considered a precursor to Osama Bin Laden's concept of establishing terror cells in far-flung places. But Hitler's were no "sleeper cells" that worked furtively, assuming a slumber stance in obscurity. They were in-your-face propaganda entities with teeth as vicious and visible as those of a hungry shark.

Cells were headed up by an *Obergruppenfuehrer* or chief honcho whose minions flew the Nazi flag both metaphorically and on the roofs of their homes. Anyone they deemed to be merely hesitant about Hitler's policies, was first "re-educated" and then strongly encouraged into following the party line. Then, if still recalcitrant, they were removed or eliminated. It was an autonomous system not requiring special permissions from Berlin: The perfect breeding ground for lawless thugs.

Non-believers were likely to be shot, kidnapped, run over by a car, or removed mysteriously to a distant place from which there was no return. In any case, decent thinking Germans who questioned the rule of these early "terror cells," were in grave danger and they knew it.

Father was a small-time diplomat, a Consul, under Hitler's flag, deeply dedicated to his country but wary and troubled by the *Fuehrer's* ideology. Still, not enough to have left the Diplomatic Service in protest before Hitler's plans became deadly realities. He was stationed in China, thought by the Nazis to be remote enough for one who had yet to grasp the new world order as envisioned by them. The German government was clearly hopeful he would become a convert yet reluctant to give him a more strategic post until he experienced an "epiphany" that would insure his party loyalty. That did not happen.

My parents tasted fear daily while trying to make at least a small difference for the innocent, stateless refugees who had fled from Europe to our little town by the sea. We were not heroes, for we lived to tell our tale.

Many throughout Europe were there with us between that boulder and a hard, bitter place, and then later as immigrants, carrying hope like a fragile, tattered banner while seeking freedom and peace in America.

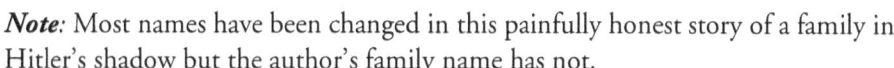

Note: Most names have been changed in this painfully honest story of a family in Hitler's shadow but the author's family name has not.

Vera Haldy-Regier's mother, Nora von Saucken, lived in New York City for the last forty years of her life. Her father died in 1966 in the Riverdale section of the Bronx and her brother, Manfred, lives in Cleveland, Ohio with his wife. They have three grown children all living in Ohio.

The author's remaining relatives live in England and Germany. She divides her time between Woodstock and Hastings-on-Hudson, New York pursuing a writing career. She lives with her second husband, James Regier and has three grown stepchildren.

China Memories: Early 1940s

In another life, in another era, I lived by the Yellow Sea of northern China in a house with a wide terrace that faced a sloping lawn. In my earliest memories, the sun always shone on our terrace and summery breezes zesty with the faint flavor of brine cooled my cheeks perfectly. There was no rawness in the air, no gusts into which I needed to lean. Memories have their very own seasons, weather born of a particular moment's sensibility.

Mother, dressed in a slender white linen dress with large blue buttons, kneels on the cool stones of the terrace and spreads rice in a thin layer with her hands. The rice blazes a brilliant white in the sunlight until I look more closely. Hundreds of small, dark insects navigate among the kernels and head towards a small dish of honey she has placed nearby. An army of midget soldiers is changing camp to assemble for lunch in the dish. They were to eat their fill and not re-emerge, legs struggling in the syrupy prison that would become their grave.

I turn away not to further witness their struggle. "*Mutti*, why do those ants have to die? They are hungry and now they can't go home again."

"It is not a nice thing to watch, *Kleine*, and I wish I didn't have to do it but we must pay the servants with rice as well as money. You don't want them to have to eat the insects, do you?"

"But they would die quicker if they were eaten and didn't have to struggle in the honey till they are exhausted," I reason, tugging at Mother's skirt to make her stop. And then she stands up and gathers me in her arms, turning so that I can face the sea over her shoulder. I finger one of her large buttons and tug till she takes my hand and holds it gently in hers. The distant pines by the water's edge bend gently in the sea wind and frame three junks that perch like resting birds in the waters of Tsingtao.

A year passes and we have moved to a new house in Tsingtao because the owners of the first house by the sea wished to live there themselves. I do not recall the move but I have vivid memories of the second home we then rented from the Catholic Mission.

It, too, had a generous terrace that faced a lawn. A twenty-five foot wisteria arbor, which was a lavender haze of dizzying perfume from June till August, formed the eastern border of our garden. A small pond shot through with flitting streaks of iridescent goldfish caught the morning light to the left of the terrace and a clump of extravagantly fragrant pink peony bushes near a small stone gatehouse completed what I claimed as my private, magical world, filled with dreams and fantasies that I shared with no one.

The entire property was surrounded by a tall stone wall overgrown with tangled vines and struggling ivy. It effectively shut out a teeming, exotic, odiferous world where small, half naked children relieved themselves in the roadside gutters and ponderous wooden vehicles known as "honeydew wagons," propelled by man and beast in consort, collected refuse at irregular and infrequent intervals.

My parents had hired an Austrian nurse to care for my older brother, Manfred, when he was two in 1935 and she had faithfully accompanied our family from Istanbul, to Vladivostok, Kariusawa, outside of Tokyo, and finally to Tsingtao. Sister Gina, or Gina, as we called her, was the center of my world until I was seven: a loving, patient presence, always impeccably dressed in a white uniform, her graying hair tamed by a small starched white cap.

She was deeply devout, fingering her rosary beads every evening and folding our hands in shared prayer with her. "Dear God," she entreated earnestly, "be with us all in these restless, troubled times and protect us from Satan's evil plans. Keep these children safe and our table rich with nourishing food." I was four and my brother ten. We children knew even then that Hitler and Satan were one.

Author at age 1 with mother in Tsingtao, 1940

Author with mother, Tsingtao

I was born in Tsingtao just weeks before Hitler's troops rolled into Poland in September 1939. The war was on and Mother's breast milk promptly stopped flowing. Her family, two hours southeast of Gdansk, faced an uncertain future and she was living an impotent world away. There was no news from home and she didn't know if her frantic letters were received. Fear for their safety was a cruel, cold vise.

So I was a bottle-fed baby, lovingly held in protective arms, mostly those of Sister Gina. Father demanded that my mother devote herself almost exclusively to him and the supervision of the household and ten servants we had in the early years. Chinese help was cheap, untrained, in need and willing. Mother, being a perfectionist, had her hands full training our help in the ways of sanitary service. Disease was rampant, dysentery a daily danger with houseflies alighting alternately on human waste in the streets and our food on the table. Hands were routinely washed in pure alcohol, water boiled endlessly and food cooked till it was limp. Vegetables were a thing to be endured not savored.

Despite all precautionary measures, I contracted amoebic dysentery when I was seven. For days I was not able to keep either food or fluid within me, was bedridden and plied with pills and potions that finally took hold and saved my life. Dehydration was a serious threat but I was kept at home rather than brought to the German *Faber Clinic* thought to be less than perfectly sanitary since the nursing staff was partially Chinese. Such assumptions were born, in part, of irrational fears but we were living in an era of multitudinous threats, which spilled over to color nearly every facet of life.

"What did you put in your mouth, *Kindl?*" Gina asked me repeatedly, her hands needlessly fussing with my covers and pulling them up higher than I wanted.

"I didn't eat anything," I replied irritably while searching my mind for a forbidden food that was never in reach under her watchful eye.

And then I remembered. "I licked some of the dew drops from the leaves of the tree by the front door," I confessed. "The blossoms were out and I wanted to suck the nectar from the little flowers," I trailed off. The old acacia tree by the front door was my favorite. Its lower branches were just within reach and I loved plucking the waxy blossoms to savor the sweet honey they harbored within. To still my thirst, I drank the dew. It was one of my secrets, never confessed till that day of inquisition.

"Well, that explains it all. You should not have done that. Flies that sit on nasty, dirty things also like dew and blossoms. That is what made you sick," Gina said with unwavering certainty, her brow furrowed and her softly blue eyes just a shade darker with concern. I preferred their lighter, sunnier hue, the color of spring skies tempered with wispy clouds.

She bent lower over me and I saw her lips move in silent prayer. Always God was with her and she made sure He didn't overlook Manfred and me. Of that I was certain.

Memories are very competitive, like race horses, always fighting to be on the rail, to make it to the finish line first. They don't appear in logical, linear time but rather in the order of their importance. So, here's what crowds the rail next:

I must have been about six when I decided to free my pet canary from its bamboo cage and confide how much love I felt for it. Gina was downstairs preparing hot chocolate and sugared, buttered sandwiches for the obligatory, unwelcome afternoon tea for which I never had an appetite. Manfred was in the garden, trying to capture butterflies in a net. I stepped uncertainly onto a stool by the cage, opened its door and reached for the tiny creature that chirped unceasingly most of the day. Its song was reassuring, a constant that spoke of predictability and certainty in a bewildering world.

"Oh, how much I love you, little one," I uttered, feeling an aching constriction in the middle of my chest. I squeezed the downy yellow bird, needing to release the pang of love in the middle of me. The bird grew very still and as I opened my hand to gaze at it closely, it fell to the floor with a dull, sickening thump. And there it lay motionless, pale and forlorn on the pitiless wooden floor of the nursery.

Horrified, I scooped it up and tore down the stairs to find Gina, wailing in utter despair as I realized that its song had ceased forever at my hand. I cried till there seemed to be no tears left, all the while begging Gina to "put the bird back together again."

"*Kindl*, I think you loved that birdie too much. You didn't mean to harm it, I know. It is now with Jesus and Mary in heaven where it is very happy," she consoled me, dabbing at a tear of her own. "Just remember to be gentle and careful with what you love most," she added. Her words echoed as an unsettling warning in the years to come and I was not always able to heed them.

There were many milestones, of course, and a lot of them had to do with Manfred. By the time I was four, he had still not adjusted to my presence. Nor did anyone help him do so.

At ten, he was not a very independent child. Gina's attentions and those of our mother were vital to him and I must have been the supreme distraction: a small girl, thought to be sweet, pretty and still in need of intense nurturing; I was seen by him as a major diversion from the satisfaction of his needs. He resented me deeply and found ways to make it very apparent. In those days before Dr. Spock, no one had prepared him for the birth of a little sister much less depicted the event as a happy, exciting one for him.

So he started his dark campaign by telling me that as soon as I closed my eyes, a large spider would descend from the ceiling and settle on my face. Night terrors visited me regularly and it was decided that I needed "light" sleeping pills so that I could get at least nine hours of sleep every night. I suspect that I had been getting closer to four hours thanks to the fearsome spider.

Next, he took every opportunity to confiscate my toys, hide or destroy them. Each of us had our own toy shelf but mine was ravaged daily and he learned quickly that the stuffed animals were my favorites. I found dolls dull but animals utterly captivating; they fit comfortably in the crook of my arm, perched on a shoulder or resting against my cheek protectively as I fought off the spider demons before sleep. And so it was that my teddy bear, white rabbit and lion cub were abducted and imprisoned under his bed or on a high shelf within a basket I could neither reach nor see.

Gina was enlisted to question him and search his corner of the nursery and when she had retrieved my treasures, she punished him with harsh words and isolation behind a locked door for hours.

"You are not nice to your little sister and that is mean and selfish. You will have to learn to be more loving and considerate of her. She is still small and cannot defend herself yet." The latter was a hopeful note for Manfred and led to immediate further taunts and aggravations before I grew old enough to challenge him.

Gina was incapable of anticipating such logic, being protective and nurturing down to the very core of her being.

Still, I looked up to my big brother on many days and envied his ability to scale our high garden wall, toss a ball across a stretch of lawn and urinate standing up. He proudly demonstrated this ability and teased me for sissy-sitting on the toilet or potty. Girls were inferior by implication, which made playing with dolls even less attractive to me.

One day I declared defiantly, "I don't like my dolls with their rubbery faces and stupid dresses. I shall flush them all down the toilet when you aren't looking, Gina."

"That's not nice at all and very wasteful. We are in a war and can't get playthings from Germany right now. Your parents gave the dolls to you to make you happy. You mustn't be ungrateful."

"What's 'ungrateful'?," I asked looking up at her from my disadvantaged position on the floor amidst my newly retrieved animal kingdom.

"It is when you feel no 'thank-you' in your heart. It makes Jesus have a very sad face."

"How would He know what is in my heart?" I persisted.

"Jesus knows everything all the time. He has the power of God," Gina replied with deep and simple certainty.

Nearly every day Gina took me along to a small nearby chapel where the Silent Order of nuns in pink prayed. I loved to accompany her, my hand protected in hers, and step through the simple portal to the candlelit sacred space with its small altar and golden cross, flanked always by fresh flowers.

We knelt together and she bent over to tell me that if only I believed deeply enough, I would see Jesus appear below the cross. He would pass through the doors of a gilded triptych that gleamed in the dusky light of the altar as its center-piece and would bless us.

I looked hard. I believed fervently, still Jesus never appeared. But I did not feel betrayed because I assumed that my belief was simply not firm enough. I would pray and wish more earnestly tomorrow, I told myself.

I loved the stillness and peace in that chapel and the sight of the gentle nuns as they lit candles with deliberate, reverent gestures and fingered the prayer beads that hung from their soft pink habits. They embodied femininity and I felt that Jesus was fortunate to have so many lovely brides.

Gina's simple faith took the Bible very literally and she felt a deep commitment to instructing her Protestant charges in the Catholic beliefs. This annoyed my father who told her on more than one occasion to stop running off to church with us and to go instead to her closet and pray as Jesus had instructed.

Gina was appalled by my father's "heretic" exclamations and I am certain she prayed hard for the redemption of all our souls. Of course I felt very conflicted in my early faith with a clear preference for Gina's style of worship in our beautiful chapel versus my father's confining closet.

We didn't actually walk to the chapel till I was much older. Mostly Gina would push me in a pram even until I was well over six years old! This astounded passersby and family friends who encountered us as she labored to push me up the small hill to the chapel. They sent shy, sympathetic looks our way, assuming that I was afflicted in some sad and hopeless way when in fact I was only the victim of irrational anxiety over what could befall me if my feet were to touch the germs of the street.

I was deeply embarrassed and guilty as Gina struggled to push me towards salvation at the hillside chapel. I longed to run freely and consoled myself with the thought that her effort was worth the holy destination. If only we could get there without anyone seeing me in the pram! It is amazing that I didn't develop all-consuming phobias about germs.

My earliest memories of life in Tsingtao are marked happily by our beautiful garden, mostly at the second house. I see the white voile curtains in my room blowing in a gentle breeze as I gaze out the window at the cool, sheltering wisteria arbor and savor the salty air that always made my nose tingle pleasantly on the verge of a liberating sneeze.

Radiant Easter mornings return vividly with Manfred and I searching for eggs and chocolate bunnies tucked amongst the bushes and in the tall grass clumps by the goldfish pond. My brother and I exchange treats, negotiating hard for the chocolates we each love best and tumble over one another on the front lawn while Mother and Gina smile happily at our abandon. But I am no match for him and he invariably triumphs over me in the wrestling and negotiating departments. I always end up with most of the hard-boiled eggs and he with the chocolate chicks. Six years are hard to bridge though I don't see it that way. I see no reason to lose out even though my only weapon is a lot of angry wailing.

And throughout it all, there is a war that I sense just beyond the closed doors of my parents' bedroom as they speak in hushed, anxious voices. I press my ear to the door and hear Mother's anguish, which is about fighting and loss and separation. Of course, I do not remember her exact words but I remember the fear and uncertainty that trembled in her voice and was most certainly not meant for my ears. That alone was menacing like a shadow you do not want crossing a sustaining sun.

Father's voice, always strident and unwavering, seeks to reassure her with the sheer force of a personality that wore bravado like a matador in full regalia. "Most people are cowards," he once said to me when I was much older. "They can be faced down if you have enough faith in your own convictions and power."

In the early 1940s, behind closed doors with Mother, he must have been facing down the demons that confronted both of them, the fears and uncertainties that Hitler's moves spread all the way to East Asia.

An entry in Father's diary in late 1940 attests to his awareness of the sobering task at hand in Tsingtao: *"I have the misfortune of having to deal with a particularly fanatical local Party organization here—one that is regularly fed the Party Line and reinforced in the belief that Hitler is infallible. It leaves no room for even a modicum of reason or foresight. My German colleagues in other Chinese posts have an easier time in this regard."*

The fact that doors were so often closed behind my parents piqued my interest in the secrets behind them. The large, two-panel French doors that separated a comfortable living room from the dining room were yet another barrier to information.

Father sat every evening on which my parents weren't entertaining guests in a deep, wide leather chair, drawing on a large cigar or on a cigarette that he held in a silver holder to his mouth. He would tilt his head sideways, inhale deeply and blow a bluish smoke into the room while my mother sat across from him, fingering an opal ring on her left hand.

How do I know? I managed occasionally to escape the cloistered confines of the upstairs nursery and crack open one door panel just enough to peek in stealthily and listen. I knew enough to pick evenings when the old scratchy sounding phonograph played Beethoven, Strauss or Tschaikowski, thus masking the small sounds I made on my secret mission. Of course, I had to strain all the more to hear what they were saying. Fortunately, Father's voice was generally loud in either agitation or frustration. Gentleness was not in his nature in any case.

"I still don't understand why the Americans announced on the radio that I had taken my life," I heard him say one evening. A cold chill traveled down my spine and left me unable to listen carefully to the soft, tentatively spoken reply of my mother. I wanted to hear no more and crept back up the stairs on silent slipper soles to ponder what I could not understand.

Years later, I read in an unpublished, half-finished manuscript of Father's that the American radio station in Shanghai had announced in July 1941 that he had slit his wrists. It was undoubtedly an attempt to boost U.S. morale and show that Germans were losing their zeal for Hitler. They couldn't know that Father had been sent so far east because he had no zeal. He was on a sort of punishment-post.

An April 1944 entry in his diary documents the pressure even on Mother by the Nazi community in Tsingtao. He writes of a visit in his office by the head of the Tsingtao Women's Nazi Group, a social organization that sought to strengthen Nazi zeal and participation in the Nazi German community:

"I was visited by a heavy-set, unappealing woman who told me that my wife was expected to donate her time to Party work within the Women's Group she headed up. I had consciously kept my wife away from these activities and the unsavory members of

the group and I was not about to get her involved now. Moreover, I disliked this uncouth woman for her Nazi propaganda at the German Faber Hospital where she was the head nurse and tried to indoctrinate the other nurses and doctors with Nazi propaganda. As she slouched ungracefully into an easy chair across from my desk, I lost all patience and hissed at her, 'Hands off my wife and out of here!' She was the same person who had reported to the head of the Local Nazi Group that my wife had been seen greeting Jews in the street and, horror of all horrors, even speaking with them."

From his writings, I was able later to piece together much of what I gleaned in confounding fragments as a small child. The less I understood then, the more I felt deeply unsettled and under threat. Single days that brought sunshine and romps on the lawn, trips to the chapel of the pink nuns, or brief forays with Gina to the produce market in town, were solid ground on which to venture forth. Hushed voices and whispered words brought with them the threat of change, uncertainty and impermanence, for how could we stay forever where danger seemed always to lurk?

As I write these pages today, I am dreaming more and my dreams are unsettling. Last night I was riding in a train to nowhere and seated next to me were two people who were revolted by me because they felt I was foreign, different and a misfit. They gave me disgusted looks and called me vile names. I tried to engage them in conversation but they shoved me into a cramped position against the armrest on the aisle of our open compartment. When the train stopped they shouted at me and asked me to leave. I felt a combination of terror, shame and anger. When I awoke, I fought my impulse to push the dream aside and struggled to reach backwards, deep into my past to remember what might have triggered it. And then I remembered a long ago day in Tsingtao.

I must have been about seven and was attending the international American school. My mother had taught me rudimentary English at home with the help of Jack and Jill books supplied by the Catholic Mission.

Most of the children were American with a few German kids whose parents had been members of the Nazi Party. The year must have been 1945.

By my own confession, I understood about half of what was said in class and the beginnings of nearsightedness made the blackboard fuzzy. I was at a disadvantage from the beginning and felt it keenly.

Whenever I was particularly upset, I would fidget and wrap the hem of my dress around my neck, or so the teacher reported to my mother. But mother was assured that I "seemed bright" if only I could develop some self-discipline.

Relief came at recess but it was a mixed bag for me. While it was good to run freely in the yard, it was treacherous to be exposed to some of the German children with no closely supervising teacher present.

Here a small historical note is called for. Since my father had garnered a reputation for having been against the war and had numerous confrontations with the local Nazis, we were intensely disliked by them. More on that later when I return to the early 1940s.

After the war, it was no longer "convenient" to be a Nazi so these very families and their indoctrinated children turned the tables and labeled former opponents to Hitler "Nazis" in the hope of whitewashing themselves. The simplistic, transparent nature of this tactic is indicative of the caliber of thugs one was dealing with.

Back to that distant day in the schoolyard. A feisty girl whose name I recall as Fey, headed for me with raised fists shouting in German, "Your father is a Nazi pig!" I was so enraged at the indignity of the lie that I lit into her with my fists and nails, then grabbed her by the hair and managed to wrestle her to the ground. The American kids stood around in uncomprehending silence and the German children joined Fey in pummeling me with their feet and fists. By the time a teacher came, we were both bloodied and in tears. When asked who started the fight the German children said in one chorus that it had been me.

I was immediately grabbed by my collar and dragged to the huge empty gymnasium. Then the large wooden door slammed shut with a resounding bang and locked. I was terrified and felt very adrift in the vastness of the space. I fled to a corner and crouched on the floor, wondering if anyone would ever return to free me or even know I was there.

My parents were called and both appeared within the hour, though the wait seemed much longer. After I told them what had really happened, they praised me for my courage, particularly my father. It was the first positive reinforcement of my life for taking a stand and it sent a powerful message that was to give me confidence in later years. I felt how proud my parents were of me and it was the only reward I needed. My bruises and tears had not been in vain. Still, I learned that day that I was different and I felt flawed. I began to measure my worth in the inflated currency of my peers.

While my schooling was rife with anxieties, Manfred's academic path was even thornier. He attended the German school whose students were largely the sons and daughters of my father's enemies. I recall when he was about eleven that he became very sullen and silent and seemed to flare up in anger at the smallest provocation. I was, of course, often in his orbit and easy to provoke at age five, being perhaps the only person in his life whom he could handily vanquish and on whom he could vent his general frustration and pain.

It did not help that our father had very little patience and on the occasions when he was enlisted to help Manfred with his homework, those sessions became terrifying for a boy who was slow in school and intimidated by his peers and father. A failed Latin declination was enough to elicit dreadful shouting and even beatings by my father. His belt was to become a favored disciplinary tool whose vicious sting I, too, was to feel later in generous measure.

Granted, our father's nerves were on edge in those days, but it is still hard to grasp that he thought nothing of humiliating my brother in public for the slowness he showed in learning.

I was to hear later of a famous beach walk the two took on which my father was practicing German spelling with Manfred. After he misspelled the word, *Fehler* (meaning mistake, ironically) a second consecutive time, my father struck him with his belt repeatedly, shouting the correct spelling and horrifying the other walkers. It was not long till my father acquired a legendary reputation as a wild, unbridled and fearsome bully. But if you were observant and just a little clever, you also saw that he respected you for putting up a good fight and insisting on your rights and innocence. To my brother's detriment, he was not observant and perhaps already too broken to rebel.

At least my father had some observation skills because he reports in his diaries that he noticed Manfred's silent, sullen and depressed behavior at about that same time. Particularly directly after returning home from school, he appeared distraught and deeply unhappy. My father questioned him about school but Manfred said that everything was fine. He wanted to change the subject and push away the day, I suspect. But Father persisted until he finally learned that the boys in Manfred's class regularly beat him up and once even shoved him down a steep incline. He was outnumbered and outsmarted, I suspect, and must have felt deeply shamed and frightened.

Later, Manfred finally confessed that his gym teacher, while coaching them in how to throw a bowling ball, said to thrust it as though they were hurling a grenade at Consul von Saucken. Obviously, the teacher was one of my father's rabid Nazi enemies. Father wasted not a minute to head for the school and threaten the teacher and headmaster, saying that if this were to ever happen again, they would regret the consequences deeply.

I have no idea what kind of leverage my father had in this matter but I vividly see before me the way his mouth would set in a tight thin line of determination and the way his hands would ball into fists at his side when he was enraged. His demeanor at such times often gave him more power and stature than he possessed in reality. It reminds me of my Retriever-mix dog, Daisy, who can chase a Pit

Bull off our property with her bared teeth though her opponent could deliver a deadly assault in a nanosecond.

I must at this point return to the historical backdrop of our unsettled years in Tsingtao. So I shall relate a crucial event in late November 1941, recorded with an asterisk in my father's diaries. It marked a visit by Consul Wiedeman, fresh from Hitler's inner circle in Berlin.

Proximity to the *Fuehrer* had colored Wiedeman's world in tones of blood red and he could no longer bear what he witnessed daily, nor, I suspect, what he was asked to do. While he did not risk resigning from the Nazi Party, which would have probably cost him his life, he asked to be assigned to China. He was given a post in Tianjin and before taking it over, decided to visit my father whom he did not even know personally. It was a puzzling but pivotal and revelatory event for my father and was to dramatically shape his years in Tsingtao.

He arrived at our home for dinner and began to describe the new Germany about which my father was totally ignorant. He told of a lieutenant who entered Hitler's office one morning, tossed his pistol on a chair and said, "Ten before breakfast is too much for me". He was referring to assassinations that the lieutenant was ordered to execute.

Wiedeman went on to tell of Jews who were transported in cattle cars to "work camps," of synagogues that had been burned, of Jewish shops having been vandalized and closed, of arrests. The litany was endless and so deeply shocking that my father felt a deep, enduring shame for his country, he told me years later.

The most brutal details were saved for a very long walk in the garden, where no one could overhear them (there was always the fear of listening devices that might have been secretly installed in our house), and they paced on the front lawn until four o'clock in the morning.

In his diary, Father wrote: *"I stopped dead in my tracks in the middle of the lawn and said, 'But Mr. Wiedeman, then we are clearly in the hands of a satanic criminal.' Wiedeman laughed bitterly and replied, 'Mr. von Saucken, didn't you already know that?' He had certainly not had much to drink that evening. I felt a terrible nausea overcome me. That night, I could not sleep for even a minute."*

For the first time in his life, Father felt powerless—totally unable to influence events so far away, disgusted and deeply depressed over what had become of his homeland.

Mother was equally shattered and both were terrified that their families were no longer safe in a country of lawlessness and fatal moral sickness. They were not to know any peace for the next seven years.

Our immediate Chinese neighbors lived in clamorous, cloying proximity to one another and their animals. There must have been a total of fifteen adults, children and elders living in wooden sheds around an often muddy courtyard where dogs, children, chickens and a vocal rooster milled about companionably.

When I was old enough to scale our garden wall, I would watch them with fascination, wondering how they survived the germs they were purported to be generating and spreading. Life on the other side of our wall seemed fraught with danger and adventure and I was drawn to the unsanitary, colorful life that was so different from mine.

Before every meal, Gina would disinfect our hands with washcloths soaked in alcohol so that we would not contract the dreaded dysentery that everyone inevitably got anyway. The scrubbing was always brisk and painful. I hated the smell of alcohol and also came to detest the odor of 4711 Cologne or *Koelnisch Wasser* that I was doused with for extra good measure.

I don't recall seeing much of either of my parents in those early years. Manfred and I were relegated to the nursery and later to our respective rooms under Gina's watchful, anxious eyes. My father believed that children should be primarily in the care of their nurse or governess and that wives were to be there almost exclusively for their husbands.

Mother did not share that view. I recall her infrequent, precious visits during the day when Father was gone as a special bonus and I always thought she was very beautiful. I remember her slender figure in a white suit that emphasized the dark hair she wore pinned up around her head in a kind of crown that framed her delicate features. The memory mingles with a photograph of her in that radiant suit, standing on our terrace in the bright sunlight. Mother was the quiet, gentle spirit that offset my father's strident, vocal nature. Today I recall her as a gossamer *Midsummer Night's Dream* to my father's raging *King Lear*.

After the untimely death of my canary, I lavished my affections on the white rocking horse with a smart red bridle and saddle that lived in a sunny corner of the nursery. I had long conversations with Magda, shared my sorrows with her and stroked her endlessly. On her back, I rocked away my anxieties and often Gina had to lift me off amidst protests and encourage me to begin new games. Magda was my introduction to a lifelong passion for horses. They never ceased to give me comfort and, even today, the mere sight of them grazing in a pasture moves me to tears of joy at their grace and beauty.

I remember that Mother used to go horseback riding with an American friend, General Clement and a colleague of his. The colleague, a certain "Red" Hawthorn, came along in order to dispel the potential rumor that the General was "fraternizing" with the enemy. It must have been right after the war ended. They rode on the edge of town at a safe distance from the perilous Laoshan Mountains where Communist guerillas hid out and mounted sneak attacks to induce terror.

I recall one morning in particular when Mother came up to the nursery in her riding clothes—a bright green jacket and tall shiny boots. She looked striking, at once fragile and adventurous and I begged to go with her.

"First you need to learn how to ride, my little one," she said smiling down at me fondly.

"But I know how to ride very well. I practice on Magda every day," I whined.

Mother's laugh rang out good-naturedly, a clear bell in two octaves.

"It's a little different on a big, live horse with so much strength and energy. You need to be a little older and then you can take some lessons," she promised. But history was to get in the way of that happy plan.

Two years later, in the autumn of 1943, the Nazi noose tightened markedly around Father and he was warned by our Pastor of a plan by the Nazis to "eliminate" him.

Father noted briefly in his diary: *"I thanked Pastor Seufert and put his mind at ease, telling him that I always had a loaded pistol at hand and that as a former soldier, I was not afraid of the Nazi thugs."*

Meanwhile, the small Jewish community of several dozen persons was close to destitution. Their passports had been taken away from them and they were stateless and often hungry, eking out a bare existence at menial jobs and living from their savings.

My parents had begun to horde food staples such as lard, canned soups, sugar, flour, coffee, cocoa and the like. They kept these supplies in the back room of a German factory managed by a merchant who had come to Tsingtao around 1910. He was a decent, industrious man whom my father liked very much and, most importantly, could trust.

After Germany capitulated in April 1945, these supplies became vital to our survival but they were also to be essential way before 1945 to the life of the Jewish community. After nightfall, at least twice a week, my mother would slip into the home of the group's ombudsman, a certain Mr. Pulvermann, and hand him supplies and whatever money we could spare. She always wore a hooded raincoat to partially obscure her face, my father wrote. Had these nocturnal visits become known, we surely would have all been shot, he noted without further comment. There was no need for elaboration upon the obvious.

Run-ins with the Nazis had an early origin for my mother's family. In 1934, my maternal grandfather, John Menger, was relieved of his post as *Landrat* or provincial governor, based in Osterode, East Prussia. The Nazis disliked him intensely for two reasons. The first was that he was known to socialize with the aristocracy. But the second was far graver.

They had dug deeply and discovered that my grandfather was of Jewish ancestry and that his great grandfather was a certain Moritz Robert-Tornow, born Moritz Levin, who had changed his name to protect himself and his family from anti-

Semitism. It couldn't have mattered less that Moritz's sister was the renowned intellectual, Rahel Levin, who conducted literary salons in Berlin and exchanged ideas with Goethe and other great thinkers of her time. Nothing mattered other than any percentage of Jewish blood that ran in John Menger's veins. It was enough to land him in jail.

It seems incomprehensible today that my mother knew nothing of her origins until she was in Tsingtao. Years later, I learned that it was my grandmother's strategy to thus "protect" her children from racism: what *they* didn't know, might more readily remain a secret to others, she reasoned.

So, on an otherwise uneventful day in Tsingtao, one of the more rabid Nazis approached Father with a taunting slur regarding Mother's Jewish roots. My father, not knowing of that ancestry since she, herself, had never been told was enraged at what he considered hateful, unfounded slander meant to topple him.

To Mother, the news came as a deeply wounding, undermining blow and she feared it would cost Father his career and perhaps his life. Moreover, the political climate's label made her feel tainted and served, sadly, to undermine her self-esteem. Clearly, she had incorporated and even accepted, in part, the stereotypes of the day. Being Jewish, to her, was an impurity and being partly Jewish meant you had a small *Webfehler*, or fault in the weave of your being. Someone had "dropped a stitch" in knitting her persona, she believed, in the hateful vernacular of the day. The result was a lifelong discomfort around Jewish people, born, I believe, of the guilt she felt about her negative feelings about Jews.

She was never to recover from that wartime revelation and from the fear it engendered. Father called it her "illness," all the while doing little to help her heal. He trivialized her pain with that ironic designation of sickness and added to a sense of unworthiness that she carried in solitary silence.

Mother continued her mother's tradition and told neither Manfred nor me of our roots and I was only to learn of them when I was eighteen in Germany from a distant relative. I remember being quite delighted that my background included some fresh, intellectual blood that I welcomed as an antidote to the long line of my father's relatives who had married "safely" within their class, thus perpetuating sameness in terms of values, beliefs, manners and career choices. From where could innovation and creativity come, born of such nearly incestuous alliances, I had often wondered as I grew into girlhood.

In the few moments of that surprising revelation made in the shadow of an ancient cathedral in an old German market town one autumn day, I sensed a new world open for me. I felt pride in a heritage of intellectual inquiry and innovation and I gave myself full permission on that day to be different from the expectations my parents had of me. I shall speak of those expectations by taking you back to a time that precedes my birth and paints a portrait of my parents on the canvas of a very different time and society. Their expectations were unremarkable against that canvas.

Prussian Ways and Other Hardships: 1910–1932

My father, Hans von Saucken, born in 1893 and nearly twenty years older than Mother, chose to enter the German Diplomatic Service after an estate he should rightfully have inherited in East Prussia near present day Kalinengrad was given instead to a cousin thought to be more "promising". At what, one asks? By the day's standards you were promising if you knuckled under and lived life according to the rules of your social status. My father, being of modest, land-owning nobility, did indeed love to hunt and watch the sun set over the rich forests and sparkling lakes of his homeland but he was also unruly, willful, abandoned by his mother and angry. That meant that he took every opportunity to assert himself, to break the rules and to straighten his short frame in an effort to appear taller and more commanding.

His mother had decided that her husband, Kurt, was too selfish, unconventional, controversial and rebellious to live with in the harsh, cold climate of East Prussia and so she took herself to Sicily for most of the year, leaving her two sons, Hans and Reinhold to fend for themselves. Maternal feelings and selflessness did not flow within her constricted veins and she never looked back, though she returned for brief visits during which she scanned the progress of her sons with cool, detached eyes.

My father lived in material comfort in the family country home, tended by nannies, governesses, a few aunts and uncles and his older brother with whom he was to have a lifelong close relationship, colored by gratitude and common memories of a wild and free childhood even by the day's standards.

In the many free hours after home schooling, Hans and Reinhold would roam the dense nearby woods with their rifles, brazenly poaching and perfecting their skills at tracking and felling deer and rabbits. Meanwhile, their father, a Major in the Koenigsberg (Kalinengrad) Cavalry, filled his spare time with childish pranks that were undoubtedly attempts at self-assertion. He, too, was not a tall man.

How else can one explain an infamous afternoon at Kurt's flat in town when he spied a cat sunning itself in the window of an apartment across the courtyard and felt it made excellent target practice? A lawsuit followed and Kurt was fined heavily for his cold-blooded folly. His retort to the judge was, "If that is what a cat costs, what do you charge for a horse?"

Sensitivity and respect for life were not foremost on that family's agenda while eccentricity always got high marks. If you were deemed a "personality" you were cut a lot of slack. It didn't really matter what kind of personality you were, which leads me to believe that this early twentieth century, seriously repressive society was breeding a small, vocal group of renegades. At least there was an "upside" to repression.

With a paternal role model such as my father enjoyed, it is not surprising that he was to evolve into a scrappy, undisciplined little Napoleon, dogged by his short height and painful neglect in youth. Life surely seemed like something to overcome rather than savor.

And history seemed to bear that out when he fought in World War I, bravely stormed a hill in France, was wounded and captured by the French. While in a prisoner train transport, he escaped out the window and hid in the forests of the Ardennes for 3 days till he was re-captured. He was to spend nearly 3 years in captivity, certainly another thing to endure rather than savor.

Still, he might have experienced his first sense of pride and self-respect when he was subsequently awarded the Iron Cross for Bravery and it is safe to assume that military mentality took on a rosier hue thereafter. It colored the way he "regulated" matters later as a father and husband, which is to say, his word was The Law. If my shy, gentle and insecure mother risked a halting gesture of assertiveness, she was instantly put in her place, which was somewhat akin to standing in a corner with a dunce cap till you realized your folly.

Mother just didn't have a chance, right from the start. She was a mere twenty-two when my father concluded at over forty that it was "time to take a wife" and raise a family to ensure the perpetuation of his very old name.

I was always told by Father that his family was traceable back to Luther while my mother's lineage, which boasted a direct, relationship to the ground-breaking architect, Walter Gropius, was belittled. She was a "mere commoner" from a family of intellectuals, bankers and creative thinkers, who were placed in the shadows of the dilettantish, landowning hunters of wildlife that traced their roots back to Luther.

But let me return to my father's family. There was one notable exception to the horde of poaching landowners. Grandfather Kurt had a cousin known to me as Count Raczynski who was a professor of art and also owned a notable art gallery in Poznan. The gallery boasted Rembrandts and a Botticelli (my mother believes it was the famous "Birth of Venus" though I seriously doubt it), which was to play a major role in Kurt's life and, subsequently, in that of my father.

It seems that when Kurt met his bride-to-be, he did not have the money to marry her or, rather, to be found acceptable by her family, the haughty, noble Heykings. Kurt turned to his cousin, the Count for a loan, which turned into a gift. The Count was able to finance any number of projects by using his fifteenth century Botticelli as collateral, later loaning it to the museum in Cologne for handsome sums. Thus, Botticelli's work enabled my grandfather to marry his cool, indifferent bride, Anna von Heyking and extend the noble line of poachers.

"Venus" came to the rescue once again when Count Raczynski lost his 24,000-acre estate to the Russians during the Second World War. Impoverished, except for Venus, safe in Cologne, he fled with his wife and six children to Chile, a puzzling choice but he must have had some connections there. The money for the trip and re-settlement came from the museum.

Decades were to pass until my parents heard from the Raczynski family. Then sometime in the late 1950s, when my parents were living in New York, a grandson or great grandson of the art professor called on a Christmas Eve and angled for an invitation. My father, otherwise generous in his invitations, did not offer one despite my mother's appeals to his conscience. She could never bear the thought of anyone being alone at Christmas, especially not on Christmas Eve, the primary day of celebration for Germans.

To this day, my mother puzzles over my father's coolness since there was no ostensible reason for him to have resented the Raczynskis.

It should be clarified that the Raczynskis, despite their Polish name, considered themselves German as they were living on what was then German land. My mother explains this simply by saying, "Germans and Poles were always close". What she remembers is a peaceful acceptance of the German occupiers on the part of the Poles of that time. The privileged of her generation and her family would find the word, "occupiers" far too harsh because they liked the Polish people and were always kind to them as they would have been to anyone. That came with your breeding and rearing and was not condescension.

Though, buried deep in that stance, was a subtle elitism that was hard to escape when reared in the upper classes of the early 20th century. How often I heard in my childhood: *"people do; one doesn't."* We were above the fray, though disenfranchised and dirt poor after the war. That elitist proclamation always made me cringe but then, I was reared mostly in the United States and instinctively embraced social democracy. It just seemed fairer, even to a 10-year old.

Author's parents shortly after their wedding at Fronza estate,
East Prussia

My parents married on October 8, 1932 at the home of my mother's uncle. It was known as *"Fronza"* and was a little south of Gdansk and just 15 miles from the village of Smentowo, or Schmentau, as the Germans called it. That is how things were done in those days. You didn't contract with a country club or fancy restaurant for the reception. You were married in the local church by the minister who knew you all your life and then celebrated the event primarily amidst family members and only the closest of friends in a home large enough to accommodate the guests.

Mother tells me it was a sparkling day with the late apples and pears capturing the last warm rays of sunlight in the walled garden, the horses curried and brushed till they gleamed, the carriages sparkling with their polished brass fittings and the maids flushed with excitement in their starched, pristine aprons that did not hint at the weeks of hard preparatory work in the large old kitchen. There were close to one hundred guests, or so it seemed to the young bride who delighted in being with her many cousins and some of her favorite aunts and uncles.

But then there were also the stern relatives who were always ready to be critical, particularly at mealtime. As a matter of fact, everyday meals were often an opportunity for Uncle Herbert von Conrad or fearsome Aunt Felicitas, known as Lice (pronounced *Leetse)* to grill the youngsters on the day's lessons. History dates were at the top of the list of appetite-robbers for how could one enjoy a luscious pear compote when your stomach was transformed into a hard, cold knot of fear because you had forgotten Bismarck's date of birth?

Mercifully, weddings, anniversaries and birthdays were exceptions to the Rule of Grilling. The worst thing that could happen to you on such festive days was that someone straightened the ribbon in your hair and hissed in your ear that you should try for a more pleasant facial expression or not forget to curtsy when Grandmother greeted you. Thank you, Great God of Etiquette, for taking a day of relative rest, the children surely prayed.

Mother reported a vague sense of disquietude when her husband of three hours eyed all the pretty young girls between dances with his new bride. It is just the way all men are, she mused. It wasn't that he was not utterly charming and attentive to her, glowing with pride over the slender, graceful dark-haired beauty with the enormous soulful brown eyes who had just become his wife, it was more that he had difficulty adjusting to the fact that others were now off-limits. He had been a bachelor far too long for anyone's good, including his own.

In his diary, he wrote: *"I had a marvelous time at my own wedding and found it difficult, in the end, to say farewell to my wife's pretty sisters and cousins. But I also knew that I had made the most fortunate and wise decision of my life: I had won an enchanting woman who would prove to be a strong personality, filled with genuine kindness and intelligence; courageous in all of life's situations; a hardworking, excellent homemaker and, later, mother, filled with charm and very adept and engaging in social situations."*

My father's eyes, which were closer to violets than I have ever seen anywhere other than in a flower bed, made him captivating to women of all ages. They were crowned by bushy, volatile eyebrows that lent dramatic expressions to his face and, given his forceful, passionate temperament, he was always able to make a woman feel as though she were the only angel that would ever hover by his side...until the next one was locked into submission by the violet light he beamed her way. When you're not tall and brawny, you better be charming, passionate and mesmerizing and he did not have to work at those qualities. A mixed blessing, as life was to demonstrate.

Mother's Engagement Photo at 21, Berlin

Father in 1933, Berlin

My mother floated through the ceremonies and found herself wondering whom she had actually married for they had only known one another for a few short months during which their meetings were infrequent and often chaperoned.

In retrospect, my mother and I are fairly certain that Father had simply tired of the single life and had also concluded that his career required a wife who would be a credit to him and was able to hold her own in all social circles. Marriage then was still often a matter of convenience, which is not to say that he was not also smitten with the grace and shy charm that my mother possessed.

Her wedding portrait, shot in Berlin, portrays a stunning dark beauty with beautiful hands and a lithe figure that seemed to simply flow into the overstuffed chair that made her appear fragile and delicate. Her enormous soft, hazel eyes showed a trace of sadness, or was it just a girlish reticence and apprehension?

All her life she detested being photographed because she felt unattractive in a world that had made blond hair and blue eyes the gold standard. It didn't help that she was often taunted by her playmates and even some of her cousins with the refrain, *"Oh, que tu est bête, bête, bête, oh, que tu est laid."* (Oh, how stupid, stupid, stupid you are, oh, how ugly you are.) To stand out in any way was the kiss of death, particularly between the ages of six and fourteen. She accepted her sentence like an innocent, brainwashed prisoner who had come to believe her guilt even in the face of utter guilelessness.

What is so deeply sad and troubling is that the ugly condemnations and lies of her youth remained truths to her for the rest of her life despite her many accomplishments and the recognition she received from everyone whose life she touched. Such can be the power of harsh indictment in youth.

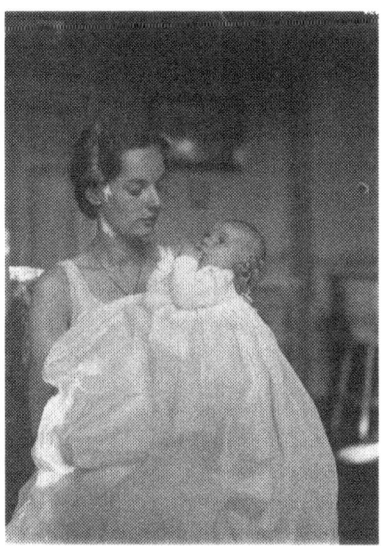

Mother with brother, Manfred, at his baptism in Fronza, 1933

From Naples Eastward

My parents' first foreign post was Naples, Italy in 1933 and it was also the first time my mother had been out of Germany. My father's previous post was in Tiblis in the Russian state of Georgia. Both were happy to live in the sun-drenched hills at the edge of town where the scent of flowers was an ever-present cloud of heady fragrance and a silver light filtered through the leaves of nearby olive trees.

Still, I think my father found Italy more to his liking than Mother, who was mildly repelled by streets that were not pristine and the smell of garlic wafting from every home at dinnertime. She retained a lifelong aversion to garlic and spicy, pungent foods, explaining that they were unaccustomed and never available in East Prussia where she grew up because they could not be grown in such a cold climate.

It is probably closer to the truth to say that anything beyond dill and parsley were not on the radar screen of the northeastern cooks and kitchen maids of her time. As a matter of fact, "exotic," garlicky fare was associated with Mediterranean peasant fare, which leads one to wonder where that left the haute cuisine of France in East Prussia's rating system.

But I think that my parents were happy and excited about their new stimulating life and my mother missed no opportunities to visit museums and archeological sites for she was hungry to soak up ancient culture and art. Never mind that you occasionally had to duck to avoid a pot of kitchen water (or worse!) that was emptied with abandon from a window under which you had the misfortune of passing. It was shocking, to be sure, but impossibly humorous as well and made for colorful letters written home.

In that first year my mother became pregnant with her first child, Manfred. As her delivery time approached, she returned home to have her child in what was deemed to be more sanitary and certainly more familiar circumstances. After a grueling 48 hours of labor, my reluctant, overdue brother arrived in *Fronza* at a staggering 12 pounds.

A rather serious infection resulted and kept my mother in bed for two weeks under very close watch for her fever lingered interminably and was life threatening. So much for better health care in Prussia! But at least she was home and cared for by a nurse and her mother. It was late August of 1933 and a chilly northern autumn and long winter made the prospect of returning to Naples quite inviting. Still, she wasn't strong enough to return till mid-November.

To help my mother cope with the new baby, her mother decided to send along her middle daughter, Freda, at least for the first year. It was also thought that Freda would benefit by absorbing a new culture and perhaps its language. Moreover, she had completed her schooling and was uncertain what she wanted to do with her life. She was a lithe and pretty young woman, blond, blue-eyed and curious about a world outside of Osterode and Schmentau with its northern chill and lack of color. At nineteen, she was impressionable, adventurous and less timid than her older sister.

While the two sisters had never been particularly close, there was no reason to believe that Freda's presence in the couple's roomy floor-through flat with its view of the sea and Capri would be anything other than beneficial for all concerned. This was to be a grave and far-reaching misconception with consequences for at least half a dozen members of the family over decades to come.

And now I must pause, as I always do when I think of my mother's early marriage years and the role of my aunt in her life. Though it seems to knock the breath out of my chest, I must find the courage to tell the story as it told itself over the many years. Otherwise, this book will not be an authentic story and I think you bought into truth when you picked it up.

There were photographs of my aunt, a budding, blue-eyed, blond and slender young woman running into the sea, seated in a garden with my brother in her lap, smiling radiantly into the camera, undoubtedly held by my father, standing pensively in the half shadow of a setting sun. My brother was a beautiful child with my mother's soft brown eyes, long lashes and chubby legs. He was well-fed, well-loved, well-cared for and doted upon by everyone in the household. For just a brief and fleeting time, life was very fine for this little group in their private paradise.

Except my father was growing restless. Mother was delicate and still needed to rest each day, especially during the heat of the day. A 70-degree day in autumn feels very warm to a young woman from near the Baltic Sea.

It is impossible for me to imagine what went through Aunt Freda's mind when my father began to surprise her with flowers, lure her to the seaside for early evening walks and then ultimately slip quietly into her room on an evening when my mother was out. It is equally puzzling to me how he justified such brazen behavior, or if he even bothered to do so.

On a visit to Berlin shortly before my parents were transferred to Istanbul, my father arranged a tryst with Freda in Berlin at the venerable old *Kaiserhof* Hotel where my mother surprised the two lovers intertwined in their room. Mother had the misfortune of needing to keep a dentist appointment in Berlin, which took less time than my father expected. It was to become the first proof of what she had vaguely suspected and her dreams shattered like fragile shards hurled against Jerusalem's Wailing Wall.

Years later, during one of the countless, violent arguments that he and I had about his affair, he justified everything by saying that theirs was a very deep love and a manifestation of *Seelenverwandtschaft*, or of being "soul mates" and that they were destined to have come together. And in the very next breath he would insist how much he also loved my mother.

The implication always was that a man such as he with the capacity to love two women at the same time was generous and large-hearted and divided his sought after attentions equitably. No one was being short-changed, in his view, much less deserted.

And as they found each other in Naples in 1933, so they sustained their bond and their meetings until his sudden death in January 1966. It was my mother's birthday when he hit the pavement not to arise again.

She had pleaded with him over many years to break off the relationship, threatened divorce, was intimidated into remaining and then simply closed the door to all her feelings for him. Mother fled into being a distant and cool caretaker of a man with a bad heart on more than one level. I know this for certain because he often complained to me of her "dutiful, indifferent care-taking," for after all, he loved her and that made it all right.

But after passion first consumed the lovers in Naples, many years were to pass. I was to have been born, grown into my teen years and become a vocal, enraged critic of my father. And he was to become Goliath to my fire-spitting David. No battles were won unless you count my hard-won self-respect in fighting for the rights of my mother.

After two leisurely years in Naples, during which my father had, by his own confession, few tasks other than tourist matters, his next post in the German Foreign Service was to be Istanbul, Turkey. He was hoping to head up the Consulate there but was only offered the position of second in charge.

In my father's diaries, he wrote of his first run-in with the Nazis in 1933 when he refused an offer to join the Nazi Party and receive an official leadership function in the local Nazi Group, as these closely homeland-monitored confederations were called. It was made quite clear to him that, even though he fully qualified for the top consular position in Istanbul, his "recalcitrant" stand towards the Party would cost him dearly. It was to do so throughout the rest of his career with the German Foreign Service. And his troubles grew like a virulent cancer. But, of course, he could have opted out of the Foreign Service on the spot.

I suspect that he was hopeful, like countless others, that Hitler was a temporary aberration in German history and would not make good on his words in *Mein Kampf.* But mine is not a book that seeks to interpret history or my father's politics but rather one that wishes to mount the canvas on which a family portrait is painted. So I will now lead you eastward to Turkey, Vladivostok and finally, China.

And history marched on. In late 1934, my father began his assignment in Istanbul while my mother and Aunt Freda packed up and joined him a few weeks later with Manfred. The grand nine-room flat that was made available there for the Vice-Consul must have been spectacular. A number of its rooms and windows faced the Bosporus Sea with its engaging, varied ship traffic and to the left was a stunning view of the Sultan's Palace. The eastern feel of Istanbul suited my father perfectly as it echoed faintly the atmosphere of Tiblis, which he had loved so much. My mother, too, was enchanted with the city's exotic beauty and they both haunted the bazaars and back alleys for art objects and furnishings.

Still, there must have been considerable tension at home as my father was always poor at hiding his feelings. The looks exchanged between him and Freda surely were unbridled and fiery and my mother probably did not miss one of them. She must have been counting the days till Freda would return to Germany and a professional nurse would be hired for subsequent posts. But somehow she could not get it done until more time was to pass.

Mother once recounted wryly how my father had asked Freda to give her history lessons in Istanbul, implying that she was lacking knowledge in which her younger sister excelled.

Of course she resented this affront bitterly at the time but was able, years later, to relate the story of her Istanbul "education" with amusement at my father's misjudgment of her abilities and his chutzpah. It must be said that my mother always had a very solid knowledge and interest in history and I am almost certain that his many putdowns were an attempt to vanquish her spirit, for she grew to be outspoken and feisty through his very authoritarianism.

The two years spent in Istanbul turned out to be a bitter turning point for my father's career as the long arm of the Nazis reached ever eastward.

The new laws that cost prominent German Jews their positions, initially targeted some seventy university professors in the fields of medicine, research, the arts and countless other disciplines. They were the lucky ones, of course, for they fled the country early and landed in Istanbul where the Turkish government seized on the opportunity to found a new university with this core group of elite thinkers. It had become a win/win situation born of a bitter, poisoned German earth.

My father, as the head of the consulate's Cultural Department, offered assistance to them and, over time, befriended quite a few of the professors, also inviting them to dinners at home. Despite the fact that many were still emotionally deeply tied to their homeland, they wisely avoided the general German community in Istanbul, which had been effectively penetrated by Nazi thought and Nazi Party members. My father's new friendships did not go unnoticed and were promptly entered into his personnel files in Berlin. Even his attendance at a concert given by a quartet whose members were Jewish, raised eyebrows and generated a hateful whisper campaign against him.

And then the Nazi axe fell. After two stormy, anxious years in Istanbul, my parents were "exiled" to Far East Russia where my father was to head up the consulate in Vladivostok for four years. In reality, the Nazis had tried to expel him from the Foreign Service but when that was not quite possible, they took the next best action.

My parents were devastated for after two such fascinating and culturally rich posts, they were to be banished to a Russian military seaport city as gray as gunmetal with few foreigners and only two other Consulates, the Japanese and the Chinese.

My father is reported by Mother to have been especially glum since Freda returned to Germany after Turkey and Gina was hired to take care of my brother. While a light dimmed for my father, a new dawn made a tentative, hopeful appearance for Mother. Now he would surely forget his mistress and she could perhaps resume her marriage. Can it have been anything other than on hold?

And what to make of a sister that seemed to have no remorse? Freda's conscience, such as it was, seemed to have been neatly tucked away behind the belief that if my father chose her alongside and perhaps above my mother, theirs was certainly the Great and Pure Love that comes to very few on this earth. They gave themselves a special dispensation based on that belief. My father favored dramatic declarations and intense feelings that raged wildly, flying in the face of "convention". Special laws applied to people of his caliber and, by association, to those on whom he conferred his favors. You were expected to accept that. And the fact that I could not do so, caused me a turbulent girlhood and eventually an ulcer.

Today, when I close my eyes, I see myself as a small figure tossing in a rowboat long ago with eyes trained on a tranquil shore in the far distance. I was destined to reach that tranquility but the journey was to take many years, given the waters into which I was tossed.

After five weeks at sea with massive trunks of food and household items along in anticipation of scarcities in easternmost Russia, my parents, brother and Viennese nurse, Gina, arrived in Vladivostok. It was March of 1937 and they had to enter the harbor with the help of an icebreaker. Snow lay deep and dirty in the streets and the rundown gray wooden houses stood sadly against an equally gray sky. Sidewalks were few, narrow and crusted with ice and snow as though few would pass on them anyway.

It was quickly apparent that it was best to move outside of town and so my father rented a modest country villa or "Dascha" about 20 kilometers from town on the edge of a patch of woods. My mother had a Russian cook and a gardener as well as a maid so life for her was very manageable. And nurse, Gina, spent every waking moment looking after Manfred who was now three and a half. There was much time for my mother to worry and there was ample reason for concern.

Thankfully, my father's four-year assignment in Vladivostok was to last a mere 6 months. The Russians were anxious to remove all foreigners from their militarily strategic seaport and they made it quite uncomfortable for the tiny, vulnerable international community there. People were constantly entrapped in situations that prompted their removal by the Russians. As a matter of fact, my father described the atmosphere there as "infused with stealthy terrorism".

In his diaries, he tells of a German official who had an affair with a Russian woman who then claimed she was pregnant. When her lover arranged for an abortion, which they had both agreed upon, and then went to meet her at the doctor's office, he was promptly arrested by the Russian Secret Police. Such were the tactics of the Soviet officials towards foreigners. You were always watching your back in the Vladivostok of 1937.

Once, on an evening walk by the harbor, my father was arrested by the Russian secret police for no reason, detained for hours, terrorized and then released. The messages to leave town were never subtle.

On another occasion, a Russian dentist who treated him for a week for a dangerous gum infection, was unusually taciturn during the series of treatments. My father tried repeatedly to engage him in conversation because he was hungry to learn of life among the Russians of Vladivostok. It was an innocent curiosity but not perceived as such by the dentist. On the last day of treatments, my father was ushered into a side room by the doctor. They sat on opposite sides of a desk from one another. On the desk were 3 human skulls with bullet holes in them. The dentist remained silent.

In his diary, Father wrote: *"In a flash, I understood the man's distant, cool behavior. I arose, walked around the desk and embraced him, then asked what I owed him for the treatments. He replied that I owed nothing and that the Soviet state would reimburse him, adding that if I wanted to please him with something special, I should send a bottle of cognac and some European cigarettes. That same night I sent a basket with a variety of goodies that I hoped would please him. I never laid eyes on him again."*

Father's obligatory reports to the home office on the state of affairs in Vladivostok painted an unembellished dismal picture of the terror and fear that reigned in the city. When they fell into the hands of Russian spies in the German Consulate in Moscow to which he reported, my father landed on a treacherous list of those to be expelled from Vladivostok by the Russian Secret Police.

To keep him safe, the German Foreign Office immediately transferred him to Tokyo and by autumn of that same year he was on his way to Japan. But he was only there a matter of weeks before the German Foreign Service transferred him to Wuhan, southwest of Shanghai to which Chiang Kai-Shek had retreated.

The city was no haven of tranquility as Japanese bombs fell relentlessly on the town and one spent a fair amount of time in bomb shelters. My father, in his customarily reckless manner, often went to the roof of the Consulate to witness the fireworks. He had an insatiable appetite for danger and a need to always be in the eye of the storm. I have always sensed that he felt most alive and vital when he could either create a hurricane or move into its deadly orbit. Some people ward off depression that way. Perhaps he was one of them.

Meanwhile, Mother who had been ensconced with Manfred and our nurse in a mountain resort several hundred kilometers northwest of Tokyo called Karuizawa, remained there rather than be exposed to the bombings. She tells of very cold nights, searches for wood and kindling to stoke their lone stove, and meals she learned to cook on a Hibachi. She lived a solitary life among the pines with Manfred and Gina and reported feeling safe in her remote hideaway though she must have been anxious about the welfare of her husband. Mother was just twenty-eight and nothing in her new world was even remotely familiar.

This separation of 10 months until Father could transfer his family to his next post, Tsingtao, was a wild and free time for him and enabled him to relive his bachelor years as only he knew how to do. He was careful not to record any of his adventures in his diaries but over the years, my mother learned of some of his affairs.

In reckless moments, often after several shots of Russian vodka, for which he never lost his taste, he would slyly and with some pride and vanity, mention a beautiful Chinese girl, or a fiery Russian lady that captured his imagination if not his bed. A hasty reassurance that my mother was always to hold first place in his heart helped her stay the course with him. I suspect that, as a mother, she had also shifted her priorities to keeping the family together and helping shepherd it out of the turbulence that seemed to follow them like the winds of March tumbling the tough, surviving leaves of autumn.

China: The Pivotal Years Till 1948

Then in August 1938, my family arrived in Tsingtao, that splendid little city by the Yellow Sea across from the southern tip of Korea. Being in the province of Shandong, the climate was temperate—warm in the summer and not too cold in winter. As a matter of fact, wealthy Chinese often made it a vacation destination in the summer, as did foreigners from large cities all over China.

They arrived just 3 months before Crystal Night (*Kristallnacht*) on which over 90 Jews were murdered and more than 30,000 arrested in a satanic rampage that destroyed Jewish shops and synagogues in Germany. The event was made to look as though the German citizenry had simply gone mad with anti-Semitism but in reality it was as much the initiative of Josef Goebbels, Hitler's Propaganda Minister and right-hand henchman. The Nazis hoped that it would stimulate a widespread exodus of Germany's Jews.

It sounds quite incredible today, but my parents got no news at the time of that terrible night. They also received virtually no news from the home office that might indicate what Hitler was up to. It was not until Consul Wiedeman's visit in late 1941 that my parents fully recognized Germany's dark mission.

Tsingtao was an easy transition to the Far East for my parents, given the German imprint that had marked it since the turn of the twentieth century. The hillsides were dotted with neat, red tile-roofed villas built by Germans who had nurtured the verdant gardens that surrounded them and built walls to shut out the poverty and rivulets of sewage that sent up a fierce stench from the streets beyond their borders. There was a German hospital, a Catholic cathedral, a Protestant church and a German consulate built of a reddish stone and embellished with a useless turret that looked foolish and discordant, overlooking a bustling outdoor food market that sold everything from cats and rats to cabbage and melons.

A racetrack near our house drew mainly Europeans, although the Chinese penchant for gambling attracted a respectable number of locals as well. To my parents, the track was no more than a way to indicate to visitors where we lived. But I always liked the idea that horses were nearby. I would have preferred being close enough to smell their droppings and hear them munch hay but I was not rewarded with such proximity nor was I ever taken there by Gina or my parents. Chances are, the barns were seen as a haven for germs.

Much of what was colorful, exotic and of intense interest to me was, sadly, off limits. On the rare occasion that Gina wheeled me to the center of town in my pram, I longed to escape my wheeled prison and run among the food stalls, touch the plump, deep red tomatoes and grasp the sticky, fly-infested grapes that made me think of marbles.

Many an absorbing hour was spent playing marbles with Manfred when my fingers were finally agile enough to propel them across our stone terrace. Mostly I had poor control and sent my marbles over the edge and into the bushes, which gave Manfred cause to taunt me and send me scurrying into the underbrush to retrieve them. They always looked precious to me, like rare jewels, and I especially liked the pastel colored ones with cloudy patches of white that allowed the sunlight to shine through.

But I was careful to keep my preferences a secret, fearing that he would take my favorites from me. His companionship had ceased evoking trust and I accepted his nature as a fact of life that I didn't ponder. Remarkably, I did not distrust others until they gave me cause. For early on, I saw Manfred as standing apart from the world I knew: a parenthetical fact that seemed to have wandered into a sentence for no reason I could discern but still had to be reckoned with.

I try repeatedly to conjure up more memories of Father in my early years but Gina remains the central focus point of those years with fleeting, bittersweet glimpses of Mother—bittersweet for my longing to have her with me more.

"Why must you be in the nursery when we have Gina for the children?," Father would ask her with unmistakable impatience in his voice. "I did not marry a nursemaid," he once added when I was old enough to understand that children clearly were not a priority for him. At that point I was also old enough to wonder if Mother was a priority for him when there were weekly letters to Aunt Freda ready for posting on the hall table. On the envelope he always wrote in large letters, "Via Siberia," the route all mail to Europe took during the war years.

Siberia sounded very exotic and distant to me, a mysterious, cold country that seemed an unlikely place from which letters were transferred westward. One day I hauled out Father's large, leather-bound atlas and leafed through the yellowing pages in search of Siberia. Gina came to the rescue, pointing also to Vladivostok and telling of the gray city by a gray sea where she had cared for Manfred before my birth.

"Does Aunt Freda live near Vladivostok?," I wondered. And then, "Why do so many letters go to her?" It was as much a mystery to Gina as to me and she answered that it was very important during a war to be in touch with one's family. "I wish I knew where my brother now lives. I have not heard from him in several years," she trailed off, allowing an uncharacteristic furrow to form between her brows.

But the mystery only deepened on the evenings that I heard Father speak Freda's name and Mother reply in an impatient tone, "It must stop. She is married now and has a child."

What should stop? Why was there a veiled unhappiness in our house that seemed to have nothing to do with the war? No matter, I had Magda and on her, rocked away the vague uneasiness that found a frequent home in the pit of my stomach.

Perhaps it was that dis-ease that often robbed me of an appetite. Meals were something to be endured, not in small part because everything had to be eaten, no matter how copious the amount. Carrots were particularly distasteful, being sweetened cloyingly with a sugar glaze I hated. Meat was plainly inedible, in my view, and seemed to increase in volume the more I chewed. I begged not to finish it but was always told it would make me very strong and tall, two qualities I was quite indifferent to in the face of their cost to my tired jaws.

I remember a singular occasion when we were all invited out to dinner by Russian neighbors who lived up the hill from us. I must have been nearly eight because Gina had already left us to return home to Vienna on one of the American repatriation boats. Babysitters were clearly not available. But I will get to her departure shortly.

We were seated around a large round table in a dusky room lit mainly by numerous, smoking candles. I sat near a radiator under a window whose heavy velvet curtains were drawn against a cold night. An elderly Chinese servant passed around a large platter at whose center a hulking chunk of meat dwarfed a ring of carrots and potatoes. A carafe of red wine made the rounds of our table and tall glasses of milk were placed at Manfred's and my places.

My stomach lurched at the sight of the meat and carrots and I felt a lightning bolt of panic rise to my throat. How would I ever dispose of the meat? Mother placed a sizable chunk on my plate, as she was seated next to me, then proceeded to cut it into what she perceived as bite-size pieces. I had been coached before arrival to be polite, observe my best table manners and finish what was on my plate.

I chewed and ground and moved the leathery mass about in my mouth, finally tucking it into a cheek, hoping it was not too visible there. Then I scanned the table from under half-lowered lids to find a moment when no eyes were on me. A candle flickered, the radiator clanked gently and I swiftly deposited the soggy wad between the wall and the radiator. Relief took the form of a slack, free cheek that evening and I settled into my potatoes, mashing them as deftly as I could with my fork.

On the way home, I felt guilty and ashamed. I had been admonished too often not to waste food, that there were millions of people starving in Europe while our plates were always generously filled.

"*Mutti*, I have done a bad thing," I whispered in a soft voice so that Father, in the front seat, could not hear.

"It can't be that bad, *Kleine*," Mother said with an encouraging smile. "Tell me what bothers you."

"I couldn't eat my meat and I put it behind the radiator when no one was looking. Maybe a mouse will find it and it will be gone before someone finds it."

"*Du kleines Luder,*" (you little rascal), she said with a smile only half concealed. "It was not a very tender meat but I don't think you tried too hard either. I do hope a mouse finds it and not our hosts…" And that was, mercifully, the end of that topic.

For Manfred and me, the summer of 1945 passed swiftly into fall. I was memorizing English words, learning punctuation and struggling with arithmetic at home with Mother. She had obtained Jack and Jill books from the Catholic Mission and I remember reciting newly acquired words while she ironed baskets of laundry in the summer heat.

Life in those books seemed idyllic: all white picket fences and little red wagons with dogs nipping happily at the heels of freely romping children. The multiplication tables Mother pounded into me that summer were infinitely less engaging and made absolutely no sense to me having been learned strictly by rote. I learned them by their sound: Six times seven repeated often enough sounded like forty-two, no more, no less.

Manfred spent the summer and early fall haunting the nearby woods with his BB gun, an American friend in tow. He was twelve and his friend Robin was about his age, as I recall. Then one day, tragedy struck and Manfred's gun, handled carelessly, sent a pellet into Robin's left eye and took its light.

I don't recall any details but remember feeling frozen with fear and horror, trying hard not to picture a cavernous, bloody eye socket. I heard Father tell that Robin was airlifted out by Navy helicopter and then flown on to Hawaii for an operation and the implantation of a glass eye. We never saw him again nor did we hear anything further about his life after the accident.

I can only conjecture today what the tragedy did to Manfred's view of himself. I never dared to bring up the incident in all these many years. His state of mind always seemed far too fragile to withstand revisiting that distant, dark day. If he was withdrawn before, he became an inscrutable, masked and lonely presence after the accident.

Increasingly, Manfred and I had less and less in common, although I do remember one warm, companionable autumn day with him when a small bird decided to make its home on our wide terrace wall. It was to be one of the last times that I felt a bond with him as we both marveled and thrilled at the attachment the bird formed to us over many happy days.

He named it Nicky and we fed it breadcrumbs, which was undoubtedly the chief reason it kept returning. But one day it took flight not to ever return again. We were both sad and I remember searching an empty sky for Nicky until the last leaves had fluttered to the ground to make a golden carpet on our front lawn. There was no one left to rake them and I was not displeased.

Manfred incorporated the experience into an essay he had to write for school. It started, "Peep, said the little bird and then flew away." He left it at that as though he had nothing more to say about the subject. He had always tended towards closing doors on disappointment and pain, leaving both woefully unexamined and unresolved.

September arrived with the balm of Indian summer and it brought the first welcome American troops. Of course, I could see none of the political implications but I was looking with the wide-eyed wonder of a six year old at groups of Marines and naval personnel who had parked themselves at the bottom of our road in the midst of a circle of trucks and jeeps. To me it appeared they were fixing our muddy, unpaved road but they might just have been setting up a watch post.

They also seemed quite often to be preparing food and opening rations that looked enticing and exotic. My first taste of American food was a small bowl of tapioca pudding topped with pineapple chunks, offered by one of our local Marines, that I found deeply disappointing. I liked the pineapple but the tapioca with its funny little "eyes" peering at me, was mildly revolting. Still, it was American and I was poised to exalt this cuisine to culinary heaven. As a matter of fact, anything American had an instant ticket to Nirvana or at least, a VIP status in heaven.

My next encounter with American troops occurred when Gina wheeled me down our road on the way to the beach one early October morning. A young Marine, appearing very old to me at the time, stepped forward and greeted us with a friendly smile. He leaned over my carriage and stroked my hair, speaking funny words that had a soft and drawly sound. I liked him instantly and asked Gina if we could stay a while and meet the others. That was fine with her and we smiled a lot since Gina could not speak a word of English and I was yet too uncertain to utter my newly acquired, limited treasure of words.

In my memories, my first encounter with Americans is always associated with sweeping change, some of it promising. But in the autumn of 1945 there were disturbing changes as well.

The house we lived in was owned by the Catholic Mission, which, after the German surrender, promptly raised our rent considerably. I will resist speculating about a possible link between these occurrences. Perhaps they were simply hoping we would move out. It cannot have seemed a badge of honor to house Germans that year.

Now, with no more income, my parents sought ways to lower costs and generate a bit of money. Father took the train to Peking and sold some of our ancient Chinese bronzes and a bit of silver.

Next, we moved to the upstairs floor of our house and rented out the ground floor to a young couple, which was sent by UNRWA (United Nations Relief and Works Agency) to help the refugees in any way they could. Happy and Bill were American and in their mid to late twenties. They were always cheerful and filled with zeal and idealism—just what we all needed in that early post-war time.

They loved living in our comfortable stucco home with its lush garden, albeit now unattended as we no longer could afford a gardener. Our gatehouse, too, was now without an attendant so we kept the large iron gate locked at all times. Looting and vandalism were on the rise and the tall stone wall now became at least a small comfort in that it delayed intruders.

Happy had the kitchen to herself and we bought a small kerosene stove on which Mother prepared simple meals upstairs on the landing where our flour and sugar chests were also housed.

Not surprisingly, our mouse population grew as they discovered tiny food rests and crumbs near the stove. Nighttime became even more terrifying for me as they scurried noisily across the floor outside my room…and into my room under the old door that didn't properly meet its threshold. In the silence of a black, moonless night, a scampering mouse can thunder ominously in the ears of a young child.

Mother was also not fond of mice, day or night. She recounts an afternoon when she pursued a mouse under Happy's bed with a broom. As she lay on the floor, her skirt hiked and her head under the bed, Happy came home and surprised her in that unseemly position. "Darling Mrs. von Saucken," she exclaimed, "what *are* you doing under my bed?"

Their laughter quickly erased all embarrassment and served to bond the two young women who were surely only about eight years apart in age.

German Consulate in Tsingtao

In those first post-war months and just weeks before the dissolution of all the Nazi groups in Tsingtao, the Nazis plotted one last time to eliminate my father, including our friend, Pastor Seufert and the Jewish Dr. Eitel who headed up the Faber Hospital where I was born and delivered by him. My father was tipped off about a plan to kidnap us all by Tsingtao's Chinese Chief of Police, a Russian by birth named Malnikoff.

It is unclear what Malnikoff's motivation was, but one can assume that Father had been on good terms with him for quite some time due to their Russian cultural ties. My father never missed a chance to practice his Russian and to speak of his fond memories of Russia and the wild Caucasus mountains he had loved so much. It was a love that stood outside of politics.

We were to be abducted in the night and flown to Shanghai where we were to simply mysteriously disappear. My father's diaries indicate that he was not surprised. It made his demeanor quite icy and I see before me the way his mouth would pinch into a tight line that dipped at the corners. No doubt his fists clenched, as they did so often throughout his life. Father's fists were always the hallmarks of an enduringly contrary nature.

Why we were spared, or why the Nazis simply couldn't pull off the plot, I will never know. Perhaps they got cold feet after my father got the word out that he was never without his pistol and would have no compunctions about pulling the trigger. Thugs are often cowards in disguise, as are bullies.

Father immediately approached one of his German friends who had tentative, ambivalent ties to the Nazi *Obergruppenleiter* or head of the local Nazi Cell Group, letting him know of the plot. He was genuinely appalled and let the lingering Nazi community know that my father was on the alert and had received Chinese police protection, along with the others who were targeted. Again, bullies morphed into cowards. The game was up for the Nazis and their local groups but their venom sputtered to a slow, reluctant halt.

Father writes of one final confrontation with the local Nazi thugs. The day was May 5, 1945 on the occasion of a memorial service for Hitler, which Father was still obliged to attend.

"While I had to attend, I declined to speak and was one of the first to leave the room and head for the exit via a flight of stairs. Immediately I was accosted by two Nazi rowdies, the brothers Geschke, who grabbed my arms, one on either side of me, and started to push me down the stairs, shouting, 'now you can go to your Jew-friends!' The fall would surely have killed me and there was little I could do to resist so I shouted at them, 'Have you lost your minds completely?' It startled them and they let go long enough for me to escape. I immediately let the word get around town that if anyone dared touch me again, I would shoot them on the spot. They all knew that I was very serious."

I was seven when a short, plump, officious Chinese gentleman appeared at our home one afternoon to announce that all our furnishings now belonged to his government. My father's diary indicates that it was February 1946 but I only remember a cold, damp day and Mother wrapped in a shawl against the unaccustomed chill of our under-heated house.

Coal was hard to come by and there was no one left to stoke the faint stove fires downstairs other than Mother. These were not duties my father was familiar with or adept at executing nor was he motivated to do so. Strangely, to him this was woman's work; men were charged with thinking in his world. So, in her customary manner, Mother took charge and did what needed to be done being ever the practical one. She never complained nor did we thank her for her efforts. But in those years, no one seemed to have time for niceties, which does not mean that her efforts were not appreciated. She always brought us warmth, it seemed, and I thanked her silently as she bent over the heaps of ashes that gave off a bitter smell till she added coal and lit the fire.

The Chinese official moved confidently through our rooms with Mother scurrying behind him. He placed stickers with Chinese lettering on each item—chairs, tables, sideboards, sofas, stools—while Mother entreated him to place them on the underside of each item so that we could pretend they were ours till their actual confiscation. We were made to feel grateful that we could use their newly acquired property till we finally left. I still wonder why the Chinese official didn't cart it all out that very day.

My father was furious over the confiscation and vowed that nothing of ours would fall into Chinese hands. To that end, he waited till we were about to leave the country, then hacked up all the furniture in our garden and set it afire. I just remember the incongruous rising of smoke against a clear blue sky and an unsettling feeling in my stomach that told me not to ask any questions.

Not a smart move of Father's for this caused quite a stir, if not to say rage, among the local Chinese officials. They fined Father $1,000 for "their" loss before allowing us to finally leave China in 1948. It was a small fortune to us at a time when we were about to set sail into an uncertain future with only transit visas and no income for an indefinite period. The event was described as "*unverschaemt*" or shameless in his diary. It was what he might have said of a young child that had been disobedient.

But my parents still had another two anxious years till our departure in early 1948 while trying to secure entry visas to a number of countries: Australia, New Zealand, Chile, Canada, Uruguay, Argentina, Santo Domingo and, of course foremost, the United States.

Predictably, German nationals were low on the long, sad list of refugees seeking a new home and we were turned down everywhere despite the efforts of good friends my parents had made amongst the Americans in Tsingtao, who recognized Father's documented resistance to Nazi policies. There were few Germans, I suspect, on whom there were no files.

And then there was also the matter of obtaining exit visas from the Chinese who extracted handsome sums from foreigners for the privilege of leaving behind almost all of their belongings before departing. We were relatively fortunate as Father had sent out some of our silver and art objects with a British Consul and a Swiss representative of the Red Cross, both of whom had received safe passage to Europe and Canada and had promised to return the goods when we were safely settled somewhere to receive them.

My father writes that part of our possessions disappeared unaccountably, allegedly having been passed on to a third party for "safe-keeping," if that is what one calls absconding with valuable objects belonging to refugees. Surely it was easier to justify deceiving Germans after World War II than deceiving most anyone else other than the Japanese.

But what do children know of all that? As I search my memory for the events of those last two years, I mainly recall my night terrors, prompted in part by the gnawing, scurrying mice, Manfred's increasingly vexing, taunting behavior towards me and our parents' anxious voices in the evening behind closed doors after the lights were turned off in my room.

I did regular battle with the imaginary spider Manfred promised would crawl all over me after I fell asleep and the canny way he would tell stories to Gina and my parents about my alleged misdeeds. In a diary that I began that year, I wrote: "All about Manfred: Sometimes I like him, sometimes I don't." I had just learned about punctuation, including colons and the need to introduce "weighty" topics before commenting on them. I also learned about ambivalence that year and that important things are not always clearly revealed. I had nothing more to write on the topic that day.

One large event stands out in my memory of the last China years and that is the departure of Gina. She had chosen to return to Vienna, having also reached retirement age. As a matter of fact, she must have been about sixty-eight when she left us on one chill spring day in 1947. Repatriation boats had been leaving Tsingtao on a regular basis since June of the previous year and if one had procured the proper exit and entry papers, room could be found on board these largely American military vessels.

I knew that I was supposed to be happy for her after the many years she had given to Manfred's and my care but all I was able to muster was a fleetingly brave face that dissolved into a free-fall of tears. There was a terrible finality about her departure—the sense that we would never meet again and the certainty that we would always live on different continents.

Continents themselves meant little to me at age eight except that I knew large oceans lay between them and the boat trip would be a very long one.

On the day she left, she looked strange to me in her only set of street clothes, for she had always worn a white nurse's uniform and white starched small hat that restrained her wispy, graying hair. It was the professional, sanitary thing to do and she was nothing less than the perfectly trained, responsible children's nurse who took great pride in her professionalism right up until her last day of work.

She carried only two small leather suitcases, filled mostly with her prayer books, Bible, collection of photos of her years with us, and her sensible cotton under-wear. I had watched her pack through my tears and seen that she, too, battled sadness as she dabbed at her ruddy, moist cheeks with a delicately embroidered white hanky. But she was also excited and seemed a bit nervous, undoubtedly about how she would find war-torn Vienna and her brother who turned out to have survived the war.

Manfred seemed untouched by her departure. Perhaps he was even happy that she would be gone within hours, leaving him more freedom to taunt me. Gina had kept us separate much of the time to protect me from his pranks and small tortures and he resented her discipline, gentle though it was in comparison to that of our father. Perhaps I will still have an opportunity to ask him how he felt that day.

Once Gina was brought safely to her ship by a large truck-like vehicle that made the rounds to pick up a handful of passengers, life took on a markedly different quality. Mother was now in charge and she plunged into her renewed role with vitality and enthusiasm. I think she was happy to have more contact with us again.

Since Father had so often admonished her to leave the maternal tasks to Gina, whom he considered to be our sole caretaker, she now had a justification for exer-cising her motherly instincts. What a joy for me! And how hard it must have been for him to give up some of his time with her. Father had always been spoiled by women, except by his own mother.

Today, if I had one guess to make, I would say that our father spent an entire life-time seeking in women what he did not receive from his own mother. Over the years I decided that a hungry man at a lavish banquet deserves more pity than condemnation.

Time was beginning to run out for us in China and I felt increasingly unsettled. Our unpaved, muddy street that led right to the sea was comfortingly familiar and I wanted it to remain unchanged forever. I loved to hear the rooster crow next door and see the chickens scurry across the yard on the other side of our garden wall, which I could now scale handily. There were numerous mangy but sweet looking dogs that roamed the neighboring yard and chased the chickens in sporadic playfulness. Mostly, however, they were too tired and hungry to run after anything but the promise of a modest meal.

The Marines at the end of our road seemed to have become a permanent fixture and a very welcome one at that. I always waved to them as I headed down our road and hoped I'd be invited to join them, which mostly occurred.

I know today that they were young, that is, well under thirty, though they seemed quite old to me then, as they would have to most children my age. They seemed to feel drawn to Mother and me, perhaps because we reminded them of their familiar western world.

They were surely homesick in this very unsettling Chinese environment with Communist guerilla forces firmly lodged in the Laoshan Mountains, just 20 miles from the center of Tsingtao.

Communist guerillas had killed and dismembered several American troops in the early months of the U.S. occupation, a fact that I had overheard one evening while listening at the great wooden door to the living room. My father sat there nightly in his large leather chair and smoked endless foul smelling cigarettes while pondering the day's events with Mother.

The word "guerilla" conjured up a fierce black beast—a gorilla such as I had seen pictured in books. Gorillas were surely surrounding Tsingtao as though the world's zoos had opened their doors and released hundreds to lurk in the mountains, waiting hungrily to devour us all. Perhaps there was no more money left to feed them in captivity, I reasoned, for there was much talk in our house about dwindling food supplies and lacking money. We would be next to know hunger, of that I was sure.

With Gina gone, Mother now walked with me down past the Marine post, my hand in hers and my pampered legs finally free of the stroller and able to kick up pebbles and dust like other children. Our destination always was the restless, ever-changing sea with its rock fortresses, or so they seemed to me.

The sea, always in motion, lapped into the inlet that formed our crescent beach and was as comforting as a soft blanket one was never without. The constant talk of leaving, which I could not help but overhear, invested every element of my life with an endangered, tenuous quality that beckoned to be recorded in my memory before it might depart forever. Sadness and unsettling change hung in the air. I felt that everything needed to be registered, to be entered into the ledger of memory that would, hopefully, hold it fast for all time.

For what is memory, I thought, if not the reassurance of having recorded poignant moments so that they may always be with you? Thus began my comforting alliance with the written word.

It started simply and with childish honesty:

Today was a beautiful day by the sea. There were lots of gulls and so many shells in the sand. Mother looked tired and worried and I wanted to make her smile. She finally did when I asked her if Magda could join us here by the water. It's not a question I would have asked Father but he was not there to ask anyway.

My notes were on loose sheets of paper, tucked into books in the belief that no one would find them there. In fact, they were not discovered for years. Written infrequently, they were interspersed with German words and without any plan for continuity, as they were driven solely by the impulse of the moment. I was very proud of my growing mastery of English and the notes were a way to practice and show off to myself:

The other day I looked through all the papers and pencils on Father's desk. I found a very big, fat, black fountain pen. It was hard to hold because it was slippery and so big *but I practiced writing with it for quite a while and then it got easier. It feels good when the **Feder** (pen point) moves so smoothly across the paper and leaves the bright blue ink that is so pretty. No wonder people like to write. **Keine Angst.** (Don't worry) I put the pen back or Father would have punished me. He has a lot of rules and they never are fun to follow.*

Along with the familiar sights of my small world—the footpath leading to the chapel with the pink-clad nuns, the makeshift vegetable market at the end of our road with its towers of cabbages and mounds of potatoes, the goldfish pond in our garden with its streaks of living, flitting color amidst the smooth pebbles—I inhaled the odors of that world, committing them as well to a memory bank bent upon holding what was certain to pass.

The heady scent of our wisteria arbor in July made me dizzy and drunk with its sweet power. I picked blossoms and pressed them to my nose in an effort to give them permanence with every breath I took. The smell of dung left by the horses and donkeys that ambled down our road, led by simple ropes held by sandaled Chinese boys, became dear to me as yet another aspect of the beloved path that led to a cherished sea.

The rhythmic sound of the horses' clopping hooves made my heart beat fast, as I pictured myself astride and headed for a journey I could direct and orchestrate. I would gallop into the sea—but not too far—just following the coastline and looking to the shore with its windswept pines that bent inland and graced the embankment above the sand. I could sense the salt spray on my cheeks and feel my hair whipping around my head to encircle my neck. I would be free, only united with my horse in a tacit understanding of shared adventure and perhaps even a mission that awaited a fulfillment only I could accomplish.

How blissful those dreams were and how desperately I clung to them in the eye of a storm that was to eventually clear the sky of all I had ever known.

Increasingly, I fled into fantasy, picturing myself—always in charge—running faster than the wind until I was flying just above the treetops, their leaves brushing me gently and the sun warming my skin just enough to offset the coolness of the breezes I stirred in my flight.

I became Peter Pan headed for the stars on my way to the moon, where I would soon perch securely and look down on the sea and mountains that bordered beautiful Tsingtao.

With my new-found magical powers that were bestowed mysteriously by my ascent upwards, I would fix our small city to be forever as it was in those late years of the 1940s with our house and garden as the jewel at the center.

I was deeply comforted by my new powers that would be able to grasp the over-sized hands of the huge Grandfather Clock of Relentless Time and hold them fast at an hour of my choosing. The ticking and clanging would stop and a peaceful silence would settle over our small family.

"Bita (my mother's nickname), put Vera to bed and come immediately down-stairs," I heard my father bellow from his big, cradling chair in the living room. Mother had just begun reading "*Peterchen's Mondfahrt*" to me and I was leaning over the pages to see the enchanting full-page pictures of Peter flying amongst the silvery stars to the moon.

She laid down the big book and sighed, stroking my cheek as if to apologize for her imminent departure. I knew what to expect because it had been that way many times before. Obedience was, in her world, a virtue never questioned, as was loyalty. The two merged in her mind to become one and the same supreme law. She was and remains a child of Kaiser Wilhelm's time much as I am an adopted child of American flawed democracy for whom obedience was always a mindless state of acquiescence.

As the year 1947 drew to a close and autumn ushered in the cold sea winds that rattled the wooden shutters of the house and blew cold drafts under the sills, we huddled under down comforters at night and navigated between half-packed lug-gage and crates by day. Mother heaped logs in the living room fireplace and we warmed our hands against the comforting flames that always made me sleepy even before bedtime.

Father brooded and smoked endless cigarettes or sat at his desk and wrote. We never knew at that time what he was writing—quite likely, in retrospect, letters to Freda. I learned later that their contact never ceased over the many thousands of miles and the years that separated them. Every hardship lent a romantic pathos to the love they both thrived on, especially after her marriage in September 1939.

I was to learn later that she was not happy and had confessed to her suitor right at the start that she loved another and would always do so. Bravely, her husband, a man of deep faith and a generous, loving heart, persevered in the firm belief that his love would ultimately win her heart. Love often has more faith in itself than it has any right to.

Heinz was a gentle man to whom helping others was simply the fabric of his being and the best way to serve God without vestments. He read the Bible daily and listened to classical music with meditative intensity, played the violin and devoted every free minute to his wife and their three children. But Freda remained absent, though bodily present. My father saw to that with his assurances of unfailing love. He was a jealous man and worked behind the scenes and across the miles to hold Freda to him as much as he would probably have worked to hold his mother at his side in East Prussia when he was five. But Sicily had a powerful pull on her.

So, eight years passed between the day Freda married and the day we boarded a U.S. military troop transport boat on January 8, 1948 and headed for America. For the next year, my father had a bit more on his mind than Freda as he shepherded us westward and into uncertainty. Still, I think he managed at least a monthly letter to his lover even in that unsettled time. He never let go of the strained, frayed thread that tethered her to him—never gave her a chance at happiness in her new life. I feel sure today that he would have felt like an abandoned child had the thread torn.

New Year's Day passed in a blur. There were no celebrations at our house as the year 1948 dawned. Mother tried hard to keep daily life regular and predictable for Manfred and me but it was hard to trust in anything, at least for me. Life had shifted to a disorienting tilt and I felt as though I might fall off and land on unleveled, unfamiliar ground.

Still, meals were on time, bedtime books were read and even walks to the sea still took place. But Mother was preoccupied and tense, Father was mentally absent and Manfred showed no signs of acknowledging the changes we faced. He wandered off by himself and spoke less than usual. He largely ignored me, which came as a small relief for I, too, was in a private world that tolerated few additional intrusions.

A frenzied sorting out of clothes, household goods and packing took place over weeks. There were so few things we could take with us given the weight restrictions imposed by the Americans who had helped us procure a cabin on the *S.S. Buttner*, a U.S. troop transport vessel that was scheduled to leave Tsingtao on January 8.

Mother gave away all our food supplies at the end and skillets, pots, blankets, pillows, vases, glassware—everything but the furniture, which my father had burned in the yard, and one round folding table with beautiful triangular inlays of different kinds of wood. It was a Mahjong table with legs that gracefully and subtly curved into unadorned feet at the bottom. The table always gleamed with fine fragrant wax, smelling to me of lemons and faraway forests.

Mother wrapped it in soft cotton blankets, which she secured with cotton ribbons so that the inevitable rolling at sea would not damage its fine and precious wood. Her efforts paid off and the table arrived at its final destination, New York, four years later with some stops in between, without a single scratch to its gleaming, multi-hued surface.

"Mutti, it looks like you are putting a diaper on a baby," I said, trailing her steps as she completed the job.

"Yes, you might say that," she replied. "It is as sensitive as a baby that will be rocked by high seas".

"What are high seas?" I asked.

"That is when big waves splash against the boat we will be on quite soon. It makes everything roll around—but you'll be safe because we will put you in a comfy bed that you cannot fall out of".

I could not imagine what she was talking about but something in mother's voice told me that no harm would come to any of us, including to the beautiful table. It comforted me as it had always been the centerpiece of our living room, like an anchor that held down securely all I knew. The table was always adorned with small, antique silver objects—a cigarette case from Turkey, a gleaming matchbox cover with our coat of arms—an eagle on a powder horn—small silver bowls from Russia. It was a focal point that sparkled with the authority and grace of timeless beauty that spanned decades, and perhaps even centuries.

And then it was the morning of January 8. We all awoke early under a gray canopy of seamless clouds. The early mist drifted in from the sea, hung in the trees, hugged the eaves of our house and laid its chill vapor on the withered winter lawn around the half frozen goldfish pond. The fish were to be left to their own devices from that day onward.

I felt a dull stab in my chest at the thought of leaving them behind. Mother told me that fish had lived without people helping them since the beginning of time but I didn't believe her, having scattered food in the water for ours for the past several years. Could that have simply been their desert, a special treat that they could now do without? Who else might care for them? Our servants had all departed or been let go by Father. Several of them had made off by night with our bicycles, sugar reserves and kitchen utensils, "souvenirs" they felt they'd earned over the years.

Only faithful Lee, our man of all trades and duties, had remained till nearly our last day in Tsingtao. On his final day with us, I saw him brush away a tear swiftly and impatiently as I trailed him around the house, breathing in the scent of wood smoke and garlic that perpetually clung to his clothes. I liked his familiar odor and the way his thin frame moved easily and deftly beneath the baggy blue pants and frayed gray shirt he wore on most days.

He had a proud grace that lent dignity to his humble circumstances and did not ever invite pity. And when he smiled, his entire face split wide open to reveal a small mouth of few teeth, while his eyes diminished to merry slits, creating wrinkles that spread sideways to lend texture to a face that was otherwise as smooth as a wind-still lake. To slip my hand into his felt as though a rough woolen glove transformed instantly into a soft, sheltering mitten that gave freedom and comfort to my fingers. Such was Lee.

And so it was less a surprise than a poignant, aching moment when Lee presented me with a pair of slippers that he had carefully cobbled as a farewell gift for me. It was a humble, heartfelt offering that we both knew to be enduringly memorable. I carried them to my room and placed them under my pillow that night. They were with me for years beyond when they fit my growing feet. I wore them on the morning of our departure and only reluctantly changed into a pair of lace-up shoes for the trip to the harbor.

Shortly before noon, an American military vehicle, somewhat larger than a jeep, pulled up in our driveway and Manfred, Mother and I piled in, while Father oversaw the loading of our suitcases into a British truck that was to follow us to the port. Uncertainty and anxiety hung in the air since our departure could have been cancelled for any reason by the Chinese officials, right up to our very last minutes on Chinese soil.

My heart drummed alarmingly and I was sure everyone could hear its beating. It might even give us away, I worried, because our departure felt so much like a clandestine, hurried escape before a gate might fall closed, blocking our way onto the waiting gangplank.

I don't know if I imagined it or whether I actually heard our father tell Manfred and me to duck under our seats before we passed through the gates to the harbor area, which were patrolled by a Chinese policeman. He waved us through, uttering a few agitated words that we could not understand, after our American driver must have shown him our exit papers.

But the four of us did not feel safe until we had walked up the long gangplank that placed us on American soil, so to speak. As other passengers drifted on board, many of them American soldiers and their families, others of them Europeans, I stood at the railing and turned my coat collar up against the damp. The water below looked brackish and smelled foul. Rotting vegetables and other garbage bobbed up against the gun metal gray sides of the *Buttner* and beggars shouted up to those on deck, entreating us to throw coins to them.

Mother had gone below deck to our four-bunk cabin near the ship's churning motors with Manfred, she, the ever practical one who sought to set up our new temporary home, while Father and I remained on deck, hand in hand, gazing at the life we were to leave behind forever.

The deep, sonorous whistle of our ship blew its farewell greeting into the fog that blanketed us, thick hemp ropes were untied from dock posts and we began to move ponderously away form shore, sliding out of the harbor and into the Yellow Sea. As we moved around the deck to get all the views, I gazed over a sea of junks, each resting like feeding gulls on the small waves.

Families were doing their wash, cleaning fish off the back of their boats and grandmothers were stirring steaming cauldrons in preparation for the main meal of the day. Fishing nets trailed behind some of the boats and dragged through the garbage-strewn water where the gulls bobbed to forage.

Father turned to me with an earnest face and said, "Take a good look at all of this because you will not ever see it again". His grave voice, wavering ever so slightly, betrayed a subtle mixture of sadness and relief. I think we both took an indelible mental photograph of the teeming life on the water that day—one that is as clearly imprinted today as it was on that January day of 1948. I am grateful to Father for having called my attention to the moment and what, by implication, it marked.

Soon the shore with its windswept pines and the hills beyond studded with German-built villas whose red tiled roofs showed faintly through the fog, retreated in the white film of a wintry mist and we were at sea. The junks were now mere dots, Tsingtao already a memory, as life on the *S.S. Buttner* became a welcome distraction.

Father and I went below to our cabin, a close, overheated space filled with our clutter and the ever-present hum of the ship's laboring motor. Everything was gray metal—the four bunk beds stacked in twos above one another, the walls, the small sink and shelf above it and a lone table. It was the kind of space you entered and momentarily yearned to flee. We faced over three weeks at sea in that room with scheduled stops in Manila and Guam. Fortunately, we had not thought in advance of the rough seas we might be facing and they were upon us soon enough.

Tsingtao's small harbor, 1932

Journeying to America

As we headed for Manila in the next days, a hurricane began to gather strength and started to whip us about mightily in a frothy, angry sea. It wasn't long till we were pitching down into deep troughs of water, then rising again to crest gigantic waves.

Over the intercom system that blared at you from every corner of the ship, a reassuring, steady voice announced that we would be bypassing the Philippines and not landing in Manila due to the storm.

"We're gonna avoid the worst winds and seas and get y'all to Guam just a little sooner. Hang on to your hats, folks". And then music was piped in over the PA system and we were treated to *Tea for Two*, whose cadence seemed to mimic the sickening roll of the ship. My stomach heaved and a glance in the mirror showed a pale, greenish face with perspiration beading on my upper lip.

I dashed out of our cabin and onto the deck for fresh air. The wind was a fury of howling blasts that whipped around the corners of the boat and made it hard to remain standing. Swells of water washed over the railing and cascaded over the tilting deck. I was terrified but exhilarated all at once, too stunned to be sick.

Then suddenly I felt a strong hand at the nape of my neck just as the next wave crested to wash over the deck. It grabbed me by the collar, pulling me towards the deck wall of the ship. I turned to find myself staring into the face of a tall crew cut MP.

"Girlie, you were about to be washed overboard. You shouldn't be out here alone in this storm. Better scoot on downstairs" And then *Tea for Two* repeated for the third time that afternoon, its monotonous cadence a comfort as we tumbled into the trough of the next huge wave.

I dashed downstairs to our gray metal "cell" and found my mother pale as a newly laundered bed sheet but when she saw me, the color returned to her cheeks and she hugged me in relief over my return. I crept into a rumpled lower bunk and hugged my pillow as we pitched towards Guam.

There were endless days at sea. Waves of nausea. Tasteless food served on metal plates as gray as the walls, the bunks—the entire ship.

Mother went to the laundry room almost every day; Manfred vomited uncontrollably and remained in his bunk above mine, his ingested meals cascading down past my bed to splatter sickeningly on the floor. I lost the ability to eat anything and still I felt sick. I might have done a great deal better had I not identified so intensely with his nausea. I felt pity and disgust, more or less in equal parts and turned towards the wall, covering my face with the rough wool blankets that we were issued.

The heat and humidity in the laundry room were ferocious and I only ventured there one time to see where Mother spent so much of her time. Steam hung in the air and the incessant drone of the machines had an almost hypnotizing effect as the boat rose and fell on the white-capped waves that we could watch through a small porthole in our cabin. There were no portholes in the laundry room and it seemed to be on a level even lower than that of our cabin.

On one particularly stormy day, a military nurse, dressed in olive trousers and wearing a small white nurse's cap, came to our cabin, my mother hanging weakly on her arm. Mother had fainted while ironing and had been revived with smelling salts. I have never seen her as pale and I was so frightened that I trembled like prairie grass whipped by a Kansas wind. Mother had somehow always conveyed her strength in such a firm way that when she was weakened, we felt in peril.

After several stormy days, the skies tore open to reveal large, serene patches of blue with clouds trailing leisurely across them, no longer whipped by howling winds. I began to spend more time on deck, mostly by myself, seeking out friendly sailors or MPs on whom to practice my budding English vocabulary.

From one patrolling MP I learned that we had Japanese war prisoners on board who were going to be dropped off at a military detention center in Guam. This fired my imagination and I pictured small, wiry men in shackles deep in the hold of our ship. They were most certainly dangerous and I hoped they were guarded around the clock so that they could not pirate our ship and return us to China where "gorillas" would descend on us from the Laoshan hills.

I also learned that we would remain for several days in Guam and I asked endless questions about the island, learning that it had many flowers, tall palms and sandy white beaches. What could be more romantic to a nine year old than the lush tropics alive with the chatter of countless colorful birds and the nighttime chirping of a million insects? In my imagination, I hiked jungle paths tangled in gigantic vines that Tarzan might swing on, swam in a blue lagoon-like cove of gently lapping water and caught butterflies in a net that I would procure somehow from my new American friends on board. Americans always had everything, I reasoned.

At twilight on a darkening sea before dinner in the large mess hall, I stared out of our lone porthole and strained to see the palms of Guam on the horizon and a welcoming harbor swarming with tanned, dusky-skinned natives ready to catch the ropes that would be tossed overboard to secure the *Buttner*.

Of course, it didn't happen that way. Instead, on one late January morning, the now familiar voice of our announcer interrupted a lilting instrumental rendition of *Stardust* to inform us that in a few hours we would be arriving in Guam and that we could disembark for several hours, if we wished, to shop at the local PX or military supply store and grocery, but that we needed to be back on board for dinner. The next day there would be a similar opportunity.

Shop in the PX? Why would I want to do that when a vast jungle beckoned to be explored? I badgered Mother, who had planned a visit to the PX to purchase honey and to buy me a bathing suit so I could swim in the lagoon that I had conjured so vividly.

As the *Buttner* finally labored towards a small cove with just two piers, I stood at the railing, my heart a crazed drummer, and rejoiced over the imposing palms that did indeed line the shore. How gracefully their trunks culminated in a shower of long, rustling leaves that sheltered the brown hairy coconuts I had studied in books. So much richer and exotic with their harvest than the windswept seaside pines of Tsingtao!

I clasped Mother's hand as we stepped down the gangplank onto the welcome solidity of land, Manfred trailing behind and Father charging ahead as excited as I to be in the tropics.

Mother's mind was undoubtedly on practical matters making mental lists of what we needed for the remainder of the journey. She had always hated the heat and didn't care for tropical foliage. Prussian pines and cool windy lakes were too much in her blood and she often said that she found palms stark and dull with their rough straight trunks and sparse greenery.

No sooner had we stepped on land but we were accosted by friendly, entrepreneurial brown boys in skimpy bathing suits who offered to scamper up the palms and cut us down a coconut for "very cheap price".

It was instant dream fulfillment for me. I could not wait to touch and taste a coconut and I begged convincingly for Father to arrange for one of the boys to bring us down the fruit.

It seemed as though a mere nanosecond elapsed before a slender teenage lad deftly slipped a sheathed knife beneath the rubber waistband of his scant suit and proceeded to pull himself up the trunk of the palm, his bare, calloused feet curling around the curve of the rough bark, strong, sun-warmed arms hoisting him up six inches at a time. A seasoned monkey would not have been more graceful or swift. At that moment he was the most admirable, graceful and enviable being I had ever seen and I gazed upwards in awe till my neck ached. The palm tree was very high and he had to climb an enormous distance till he reached the leafy home of the hairy fruit.

Sturdy fronds rustled high above us, almost like sabers rattling, and then I heard the swift, confident slash of the boy's knife. A coconut crashed down and rolled a few feet in the sand. I ran to pick it up and marvel at its rough bristly surface and substantial weight. The boy scampered down, a wide, proud grin on his face. He whipped out his knife again and slashed open the fruit. Its white meat glistened in the bright tropical light and I breathed in the subtle, slightly sweet smell of its meat.

Coconut milk pooled in its center and the boy indicated that I take a taste. I glanced at Mother for a green light, remembering the incessant warnings about germs in Tsingtao, but she said confidently, "Here it is safe to eat the food. It is like being on American ground." Hers was the simple faith of all refugees in the late 1940s, notwithstanding that we were still thousands of miles from American shores.

I held the halved coconut to my lips, breathed in its strange sweet scent and tasted the milk. I think I expected the taste of cow's milk, given its color, and was deeply disappointed in the watery sweetness that filled my mouth. I wanted to spit it out but was afraid to offend the boy whose expectant face studied mine in the certainty that I would express delight. I held my breath, swallowed and smiled at him. "Thank you. That was good," I managed.

Instantly we were surrounded by three more boys, promising to fetch an even larger, sweeter coconut for us. I passed the fruit on to my father who tasted the milk and screwed up his face in obvious distaste, leaving me embarrassed and uncomfortable. I stole a glance at our nimble harvester and saw his smile fade as though his face were a rare flower closing and folding inward as night falls. Mother declined a taste politely and Manfred wandered off distractedly, taking no further notice of our small beach party.

We ambled on behind a group of ship passengers who seemed to be following a simply painted sign on a scraggly tree that pointed inland and announced the PX. We were now under the canopy of tall trees with voluptuous, dark green leaves, on a narrow dirt path that seemed to lead into a darker, cooler part of what I hoped was a jungle.

And then we were in a small clearing in the midst of which stood a barrack-like structure with a corrugated tin roof. Its sides appeared also to be made of metal and the afternoon sun, slanting through the foliage, glinted on its barrel-shaped sides in dull flashes of leaf-shaded light.

We entered an emporium of unfamiliar riches—shelves of tinned goods, piles of simple, colorful cotton clothing, stacks of paperback books, a corner of small wicker furniture from the Philippines, a shelf of personal care products that included toothpaste, bottles of aspirin, remedies of all sorts that I knew nothing about, Band Aids, and probably condoms, douches and a host of other things I can only conjecture about in retrospect.

Overhead a large fan rotated slowly and stirred the heavy, flower-scented air that flowed languidly in through doors, which were thrust open widely to the lush green world outside.

Mother browsed up and down the three aisles that gave generous access to the laden shelves on both sides while I headed straight for the clothing section and began to look for bathing suits. I soon discovered a blue-checkered suit with discretely ruffled pants that seemed just fine to me; I really didn't care how it looked.

Father and Manfred tagged on behind Mother, showing less interest in the wares and chatting loudly in German, which caused my cheeks to burn with self-consciousness and embarrassment. I wanted merely to blend into the colors and textures of the space we wandered—to become an entity bearing no burden or signature of nationality save perhaps becoming miraculously and instantly American. Being so evidently German, I had been conspicuous and ridiculed for longer than I could now bear. And in a comforting flash of fantasy, I saw the blue ruffled bathing suit as a great equalizer—a costume I could slip into and become recognizably American.

Mother handed me the suit, now within a brown paper bag, and I tucked it under my arm where it seemed to be safest. I resisted the urge to look inside the bag until we were somewhere where I could pull myself into what was to become my first American disguise. I would instantly assume my new American persona, I reasoned with considerable excitement and pride.

I longed for magic that day like Peter Pan might have wished for a sturdy star to ride through the heavens. America was drawing closer and would give us shelter because it was certainly a benign and loving place. It no longer felt like I had left behind a home because the promise of what lay ahead settled over every new day with a delicious dreamed reassurance. Myth and longing had joined to create a new hopeful reality.

But the shadows were lengthening and the bright afternoon light gave way to a softer sun that filtered through the stately palms and the dense underbrush in golden waves. It was time to return to our ship for the evening meal and my swim had to wait till the next day. We wandered back towards the simple wooden pier with its rope-railing.

A group of young boys lingered nearby and stared at our ship with curiosity and longing. Our arrival was undoubtedly the highlight of the week, if not the month, and the promise of a few coins did much to offset their disappointment at not being allowed to board the *S.S. Buttner*. They didn't need to stretch out their hands for coins; their dark soft eyes asked eloquently for our small gifts.

I couldn't wait for the sun to be high in the sky the next morning as I wriggled into my new suit, a towel under my arm and Lee's fine new slippers on my feet. I tore down the gangplank with Mother reluctantly in tow.

"We'll have to first see if the water is clean enough to swim in," she admonished, but I was paying little attention to her all too familiar preoccupation with sanitation. The water was a brilliant blue-green and it lapped up around the fallen coconuts and pieces of driftwood that littered the fine white sand. I kicked off my leather slippers and ran ahead, leaving Mother behind to worry about seashells gouging my feet, germs invading bloodied toes and whatever else mothers always seemed to be anxious about.

So this is what freedom feels like, I thought: The chance to outrun restraining hands and to let worried words be lost to the wind. I might well have left early childhood behind that morning, trading it in for a joyful unfolding that had been waiting in the wings. I was poised to leap into living fully. But that is only my adult gazing back decades later at the child on a beach in Guam on that sun-filled morning of promise. What I do remember for certain is a warm sea that smelled of salt and flowers, stray blossoms that floated on its surface and a breeze so soft that it felt like butterfly wings caressing my cheeks.

I wonder now where Manfred and Father were that morning. Perhaps they wandered along the beach or explored our ship now that it was not pitching precariously. Manfred had spent most of our time at sea in his bunk bed so he might well have had the urge to investigate the ship.

Perhaps he was curious, as was I, about the Japanese "gorillas" we were scheduled to unload in Guam. Somehow I missed their procession onto shore but my fertile imagination had them hobbling in leg irons down the gangplank, the rifles of tall, accompanying MPs pointing menacingly at them. Surely their departure actually took place furtively in the dark of night, most unceremoniously and without my imagined, embellished and dramatic highlights.

Later that day, I stood on board to watch the heavy ropes be unwound from around the pier posts and to listen to the deep roar of our motors fire up as the ship turned laboriously and pointed its bow out to sea once again. A bass blast of our horn signaled departure and sent a gentle shudder through the ship. I gripped the railing tightly till my fingers were white and felt an inexplicable nostalgia for the tropics I had only just tasted for such a brief, sweet time. I remember sending a quick prayer of hope out to sea that I would experience such lush, vivid tropical beauty again.

My reverie was promptly interrupted by the inescapable intercom music, this time a jaunty version of *Jeepers Creepers (where'd you get those peepers...)*. The words made no sense...what on earth are "peepers," I wondered. Twittering birds? America was drawing nearer with all its mysteries and the transition was gentle, except for the seas.

Soon thereafter we crossed the International Date Line and my mother had her birthday twice, once in each time zone. This was an incomprehensible mystery to me, too abstract, too much like grown-up magic and, I decided, too advanced for me to even try and comprehend till I was older.

It was the first of several times in my young life that I was to conclude that something needed to be put off and dealt with when I was old enough to have a better grip on it. For me, everything eventually entered its right time—a time when an event was ripe to reach up and grasp, to pluck it and bite into its bittersweet juice. I would digest on *my* timetable. And that is exactly how I dealt with the saddest event of my whole life just three years later. I will share that memory with you in due time.

The sea became a bit calmer as we neared our San Francisco destination. Every day I went out on deck to look for the California shore, no matter how strong the winds were or how high the seas. In between, I wandered the ship and asked endless questions of the passengers and military personnel. I have only a scant recollection of the passengers—mostly navy wives in peddle pushers, now fashionable again as Capri pants. There were also German passengers, a few Jewish families and the American Consul General, a Mr. Spiker, who had been instrumental in procuring our entry papers to the States. He was returning for a much-needed home leave and was to play a key role upon our arrival in San Francisco.

Mother was always in the laundry room, it seemed. Father read whatever books, flyers and brochures he could get his hands on and Manfred lay in bed in sick torpor. Those are my impressionistic recollections, which probably reflect the general atmosphere and activities of those languid, though unsettled days fairly accurately.

Square Pegs in America

On the morning of February 3, after 25 days at sea, we finally sighted land a second time and I knew we must be entering American waters. A heavy fog shrouded the faint gray line of land on the horizon and drifted in varying densities across the bow of our ship, curling comfortably around our smokestacks. The deck was wet and slippery as I ran from one side of the ship to the other and I made a game of sliding into the railing from a running start.

America! Now you saw it through the fog, now you didn't. I had seen pictures of the Golden Gate Bridge and, of course, expected it to appear immediately before us, complete with rainbow and bursts of sunlight glinting off its graceful, gossamer span. I was Alice in Movie Land and America was the Kingdom of Oz with more promise than any place had a right to have.

Instead, as we plowed onward through the billowing fog, we caught only fleeting, filmy snapshot impressions of the distant shore, which began to reveal a few hazy building outlines but no glorious bridge.

My parents joined me at the railing. Father had put on an old crushed felt hat and pulled down its brim to shield his face from the damp air. Mother's dark soft hair, which was too fine to withstand the slightest breeze, blew wildly around her face and her cheeks were flushed with excitement. I thought she looked very beautiful in that moment—freer and more hopeful than I had seen her in several years. I felt a surge of joy for all that we might soon experience. We were going to be safe at last and I recalled with a slight lurch of my stomach how uncertain and frightening our last months in Tsingtao had been for me, for all of us: a modest epiphany in retrospect or perhaps simply a delayed response?

Manfred stood slightly apart from us, still pale from his unrelenting nausea and distant in his demeanor. He seemed apprehensive and withdrawn, perhaps wondering about the new uncertainties we faced. He must have known, as I did not, that our entry papers did not allow for permanent residency and he might have felt Father's dark spirits that always expressed themselves in the down turned corners of his mouth and clenched fists. Father was ready for his next fight, I knew.

I was embarrassed about his seeming hostility or what he would have called "preparedness," being myself so ready to embrace and welcome America and expecting it to rejoice equally in our arrival. I lowered my head and walked towards the bow to distance myself and be alone with my wild hopes for whatever lay ahead. I felt the cold mist and fine sea spray and I welcomed them and whispered my private greeting into the wind: "Hello, America!"

When we finally docked at our designated pier, I was astounded by the many people at the harbor who rushed to their various tasks in securing our ship. To my surprise, I saw quite a few Chinese dock workers, which made no sense to me now that we were so many thousands of miles from China. How had they gotten here, I wondered. Hadn't we just left them all behind forever? Hadn't we said our final goodbyes?

It was somehow comforting to see their familiar features in the turmoil on land and I felt glad that they, too, had been able to come to such a promising country. They did not look thin and hungry and they weren't begging, I decided: so different from their brothers and sisters who had remained behind in China.

There was not much time to ponder further or take in early impressions because we had luggage to close up and carry, piece by piece, to the top deck for disembarkation. Such excitement, such confusion such frantic activity as passengers crowded the deck and looked for family and friends on the pier below!

But no one awaited us, of course, and I was suddenly seized by a sense of aloneness and apprehension. Would there ever be anyone who knew we were now in the United States of America? Or, would there soon be people who cared what happened to us in this very large land that began here at a pier in a harbor? My world was on the brink of expanding beyond measure and I relished that certainty like the bittersweet taste of late summer blackberries.

The next few hours are a dim memory. I was too excited and undoubtedly also too anxious to take everything in. What remains is a memory of standing in long lines in a large hall while everyone's papers were examined with painful exactitude by a grim, unsmiling man in a strange dark uniform.

Some people were sent ahead and proceeded towards a wide door that appeared to be an exit to the world outside where a dim sun struggled through the retreating morning fog. We were asked to join a group that was ushered into yet another hall for further questioning.

I straggled behind with Manfred while our parents nervously stammered explanations of our status in their fledgling English. Most of those in our group were Asians with far less knowledge of English than our parents. They were dressed in the customary blue quilted jackets and baggy pants and chattered in agitated Chinese amongst themselves. It hardly seemed to me that we were in America while in that hall.

But the most vivid memory I have of that day is our transfer to a detention center for aliens with insufficient papers to remain permanently in America. At the time, of course, I did not know the purpose of the place. What I do remember are the bars on all windows and a fortified metal door that closed behind us with a reverberating clang. I felt a chill—there was no way out, I realized.

I was certain we were in jail and for a few fleeting moments, it merely felt like an exciting chapter in a book that I was anxious to finish. This was like the movies and I was an actor in the unfolding of its events: a dramatic end to a long and hopeful journey.

The room had metal folding chairs and long gun metal gray tables that were being readied for a midday meal. The barred windows were high up and quite small, admitting only shafts of sunlight that cast shadowy stripes on the concrete floor. The stone and metal amplified every sound and there was a disturbing din of vexed voices: A chorus of agitation and unhappiness. And there was no place to retreat to and allay one's own anxieties.

Father stormed to the front of the hall where two guards with pistol holsters stood officiously, their legs spread widely in a stance of stolid resistance to the room. Clearly, none of us were going anywhere but our father would see to it that they knew we were different from the rest.

I tucked my head into the collar of my dress and studied the floor as I heard his voice boom across the room.

"We have papers that say we can enter ze United States. We have American friends. Please, I want speak to an official immediately."

"Mister, you no different than the rest of these here folks till we process your papers and background. You are German, right? That does make you different but I'm not sure that's going to help you much." A considerable understatement in early 1948!

"I want telephone," My father bellowed. I can't imagine whom he was going to call.

"You don't want anything, mister, till we decide that you'll have it."

My father's fists balled menacingly and I tucked my head back into my collar. Mother fluttered around like a bird in a rainstorm, then headed towards him with a newly resolute stride. She placed her hand on his arm and I sensed her pleading with him to stop creating such a commotion. I thanked her silently from afar, wanting merely to fade into the gray of the walls, the gray of the cold stone floors. Manfred retreated to a nearby chair and watched with wide anxious eyes. He, too, was staying out of the middle of the maelstrom, his shoulders stooped and hands deep in the pockets of his trousers.

And then Consul General Spiker appeared at the head of the room. He walked over to Father and the guard with resolute steps. We could hear his calm, authoritative voice though not his words. Father was ushered into another room together with Mr. Spiker and we stood in anxious though hopeful silence, our eyes glued on the door through which they had just passed.

An eternity of perhaps thirty minutes passed and then Father and Mr. Spiker reappeared and walked towards the three of us with an energetic, jaunty gait.

We were by one of the high windows, catching the striped rays of sunlight that now settled a comforting warmth across our shoulders. I had watched the interplay of light and dancing dust particles to distract myself while chewing on my thumb. I remember that detail because I had shredded my cuticle till it bled and Mother scolded me for getting blood on my skirt.

"Well, that's all settled," Mr. Spiker said with satisfaction. "Bureaucrats love to show that they're earning their keep. You're fine now and they've recognized your 60-day permit to stay here in the States. Boy, you had me worried there for a while when you showed up in the wrong line!"

Mother took both his hands in hers and thanked him in a voice unsteady with emotion. Father put his hand on Spiker's shoulder, looked deeply into his eyes and said, "We will never forget this moment. We have so much to thank you for." He infused the moment with his inimical sense for drama as though a camera were recording the instant for all time. But there was no doubt that his gratitude was deeply genuine. Perhaps he wanted that heartfelt emotion to be recorded for all time as well.

The family 3 months before leaving China for the U.S.

Newly arrived in San Francisco, 1948

That anxious chapter of our lives culminated in the appearance of a newspaper article about us in *The San Francisco Chronicle*. It announced that the first German officials—and the word, "Nazis" may have been in the headline—had entered the United States. I only know of its contents from my mother's scanty recollections. The story spoke of Father's duties in Tsingtao as a German government official who was responsible for the refugee community in that town.

There followed, a few days later, a number of letters to the Editor from Tsingtao families who remembered the modest help my parents had offered there: Jewish families who reached across the abyss of a terrible history to say thank you for small kindnesses.

On the advice of Mr. Spiker, we transferred over to a small hotel across the street from the old St. Francis Hotel. It was a less expensive alternative and perfectly fine for the few days we spent there while we looked for a place to stay for the next five weeks. Our visa would run out then and we needed to be on our way to either Cuba or Santo Domingo in order to await permission for permanent residency in the U.S.

Mother was quite tense during this time and Father, not ever having been practical, left most duties up to her. He gave off an air that said he saw himself as the General or decision-maker with Mother doing the footwork.

"You have such a charming way with people," he told her. "Besides my English is not as good as yours." Both observations were accurate. Father spoke with a rasping, throaty accent, spewing forth a fine learned vocabulary that managed nonetheless to insult any but the most impaired ears with its strident guttural sounds. And where Mother's charm was concerned, she was simply a very sensitive and caring person, always genuinely interested in whomever she was speaking with. She was never manipulative or gracious with a self-serving purpose and was ready to give a compliment in a heartfelt manner whenever appropriate. A deep and authentic generosity lies at the heart of her nature that still shines through in her old age as I write these words.

Mother's footwork began with a trip to the local newspaper—it might well have been *The San Francisco Chronicle*—in which she ran an ad requesting a room or two for a few weeks. It must have mentioned that we were German immigrants awaiting permanent residency because the ad was answered by a very kind German lady by the name of Mrs. Fischer, who had a large spare room in her house for the four of us and also offered the use of her kitchen.

I remember her as having gray hair and pale blue eyes. She was pleasantly plump but moved with a sprightly gait and an always-ready smile endeared her to us instantly. Her German was fluent and we soon learned, after Father's persistent probing, that she was a niece of the poet Heinrich Heine. A husband was never mentioned and I hope Father never asked in his customarily direct manner. If he did, she never held it against us. Of course, I knew nothing of Heine at age nine, though the fact that he was a renowned poet made a significant impression on me.

In my daydreams of the past two years, I was always a published poet and certainly also a writer of prose. This was not because I had a strong faith in my abilities but rather because I felt the most comfortable and comforted when sitting quietly with pencil in hand and entrusting my most privately held thoughts to paper. It was a deep trust I felt in the taciturn nature of the paper. It would not betray my secrets until I was ready to offer them up. Words were companions in dialogue with confidants, for their messages were at the same time the eager ears that heard them: to write is to hear oneself think and feel.

Mrs. Heine Fischer, as I now thought of her, had stature to which I aspired. Her shelves of books, her thoughtful manner of speaking, her kindness only served to gild my image of her and to strengthen my resolve to become like her.

"You are so thin, child. Have a little more of that fine pudding your *Mutti* made," she suggested with concern in her eyes. She stroked my hair as she spoke and when she bent down to look into my face, I breathed in the scent of her cologne—unmistakably 4711 *Koelnisch Wasser*.

Mother was meticulously neat in Mrs. Fischer's kitchen, feeling she needed to be tidier here than in her own kitchen. After all, she would say, we are refugees and have been taken in for a very reasonable rent in order to help us on our path to cobbling together a new life. And so she scrubbed the clean floor, wiped the pristine windowsills, cleaned the sparkling oven and washed the bright kitchen curtains, ironing them to creaseless perfection.

She was in perpetual motion while Father wandered about lost and perplexed over America's "peculiarities". Buses whizzed by without stopping for him because he was wandering between stops. Seeing the bus approach sent him into a frenzy of waving and yelling, "Bus, *Halt, Shtop!*" and when it did not, he shouted his frustration into the wind much to the consternation of other pedestrians who were jolted out of their reverie by his torrents. We were intensely embarrassed by his antics and he was quietly amused by our discomfort.

"Why can't I say what I feel—I thought we were now in a Democracy," he uttered with commensurate ill humor.

"Must you always call attention to yourself," Mother exclaimed in exasperation. "We are guests in this country and just now only passing through." It was a stance she held for the next half century—ever the humble diner at a rich table whose bounty she never seemed to feel worthy of.

Supermarkets fascinated Father. There were so many goods—many of them mysterious such as the selection of breakfast cereals. He would study the boxes and read the labels carefully in order to discern the use of these confounding products. Cheerios were ubiquitous and he could not fathom adding milk and fruit to small circles of grain in place of whole grain bread, sausage and cheese to accompany his morning coffee.

"This is not civilized," he declared and I confess that the rest of us were equally puzzled, though curious, about the strange, soggy breakfast habits of Americans.

Mrs. Fischer made just one attempt to acclimatize us to a breakfast of cereal but she found us only polite takers who pushed the pulpy cereal around in our bowls and dutifully finished the mush we created in reluctant spoonfuls. Waste was not even a remote option, of course. As a compensation, Mother would cook sauerkraut and sausages or make beef roulades for dinner, the latter remaining a favorite in our family. Generally, Father would suggest the menu, that is, request the dishes he liked, encouraging Mother not to neglect her keen baking skills.

She complied with zest and one day baked a delectable *Linzer Torte*, which Gina had taught her to make in China. It bore no resemblance to the powder sugar-crusted cookies with jelly in the center that make a claim on the same identity. Rather, this was a lavish cake, rich in almonds, butter and eggs with a pastry-latticed topping dotted with raspberry jam. One thin slice can nourish an adult for a day! As an added bonus, Mrs. Fischer's house took on an almond fragrance that lasted far into that night and transported us to Vienna in our dreams.

In our early San Francisco days, I remember visiting a Mrs. Schoen in Oakland one afternoon with my family. She lived in a sun-filled apartment that smelled of cinnamon and freshly baked cake. We traveled there on a pokey bus that stopped frequently and gave us fine views of the Bay area.

Mrs. Schoen and her husband had lived in Tsingtao as Jewish refugees while we were there. Her husband had died in Tsingtao of cancer in 1947 and was buried in a small, obscure Jewish cemetery that had been desecrated by the local Nazis. From my parents' descriptions, they were exceptionally fine and cultured people who missed no opportunity to show their gratitude for the food baskets and cash Mother would bring after dark whenever it was safe enough to venture forth in her hooded raincoat.

This time Mrs. Schoen could reciprocate and she glowed with pleasure and pride at welcoming us in her comfortable little flat. The smell of coffee perfumed the room and a pitcher of milk for Manfred and me as well as a bowl of whipped cream to accompany the cake she had baked graced the table by her small sofa.

We wedged ourselves in on the soft cushions while Mrs. Schoen heaped our plates with cake and *Schlag*.

As soon as we had finished the first helping, she served the next and lavished it with mounds of cream.

"You are so thin, all of you, especially the children," she said with genuine concern and Mother explained that the weeks at sea had been stormy and we had not been able to eat. Actually, Mother was the thinnest as I recall. She wore a pale gray linen suit that day and I noted that the jacket hung loosely on her narrow frame, her cheeks gentle sunken hollows below shadowed eyes.

But that afternoon the talk was spirited while memories of China were shared and an optimism was given voice because we were all safe in America, at least, in our case, for the next few weeks. Life was measured in small, precious spoonfuls in those days.

The return bus trip became a battle with nausea for me. I had eaten far too much rich food and took deep gulps of air to settle a stomach that strained against the waist of my dress. It was my favorite dress, blue with white flowers, and I was determined not to soil it. At least three years were to pass before I was able to eat whipped cream again without reliving the nausea of that afternoon on the bus back to San Francisco.

Sometime in those short weeks in San Francisco, Manfred was confirmed in a Lutheran Church, which was presided over by a German minister who was recommended by Mrs. Fischer. No doubt, she was a member of the congregation and helped arrange the necessary instruction for Manfred to catch up to the others in his church class.

Mother labored for weeks to alter one of Father's suits for him to wear at his confirmation. She did a remarkable job and her fingers were red from pinpricks and scissoring by the time the dark wool suit was ready. He looked handsome and older than his years as he marched down the aisle of the small church filled with spring flowers. We were all proud of him and our parents showed visible relief that this rite of passage had been accomplished.

"Who knows where we might have found a German Lutheran pastor after this point," Father mused as though we were about to be launched into a spiritual desert as defined by the lack of a Lutheran church. He wore being foreign with defiance and conviction. Even his God was Lutheran and did not preside in America. Nor did much else that he held dear such as chewy, dark country breads and Beethoven at any time of day.

One afternoon in Mrs. Fischer's kitchen while listening idly to the radio, a Benny Goodman number came on. Goodman's clarinet soared over the masterfully disciplined orchestra like a seagull might glide over a tumbling sea. I was transfixed by the sweet effortless passages and found myself tapping to the rhythm with my foot. I felt a surge of joy at being able to abandon myself to these wonderful sounds that were so fresh and new for me.

Just then Father walked in, stopped dead in the door and with a look of deep distaste said, "What is that terrible ruckus you are listening to? It is uncivilized music. I think the Americans do not understand real music and I cannot listen to theirs. Turn off that noise immediately."

I could not comply right away, stalling to be able to hear the end of the clarinet solo. That earned me a bellowing second command to shut off the radio; he presumed correctly that he would not be able to do so himself, being hopelessly impractical and unpracticed in many of the simplest technical tasks.

Angrily, I shut off the music and left the room sulking and despairing of a father who was, in my mind, a hopeless, selfish misfit. But I had made a delicious discovery that would later bring me countless hours of intense pleasure and lead me to explore jazz extensively and also discover the music of such American giants as George Gershwin, Irving Berlin and Johnny Mercer.

Destination: Havana

Then, all too soon, our time was up. For a full day, Mother cleaned and packed while Manfred and I moped around without offering to help, nor were we asked to. It was always hard being up against Mother's swift efficiency; it supplied a convenient excuse for our sloth. Even though she tried not to criticize our efforts when we did make them, it was clear we were neither as neat nor as organized and efficient as she.

Father had taken to writing a great deal and I was to learn later that much of that effort was poured into letters to Freda. The letters served as a kind of weekly diary of our activities (she saved them although I never saw them) and also continued to bind her to him. Naturally, his outpourings created tremendous friction on both sides of the ocean. I can speak first hand about our side as I recall Mother pleading with our father to stop corresponding with her sister and allow Freda's marriage to take hold. Their first child, Angelika, had been born and a son was soon to follow. But Father was true to his single-minded nature and never wavered from the pursuit of his sister-in-law.

Freda's marriage to the gentle, pious man from the Black Forest region, had taken her from Berlin to Freiburg, a charming small southwestern town with a lofty gothic cathedral, an old university and ancient cobblestone streets with sparkling rivulets running alongside to keep the streets clean. Tucked against the towering mountains covered with stately pines and high alpine meadows, Freiburg had become a popular resort and retirement destination. But it was also an ideal place to raise children if only more vital healthy family conditions had been in place. I was to learn later how disquieting those years were for my cousins.

In the meantime, we were on the move eastward for my parents had chosen Cuba as our transitional base from which to apply for and await a permanent visa to re-enter the States.

With no income and an unknown period of time to bridge till that might change, it was decided that we would take a bus across the country to Miami. The trip was said to take five days on a bus line called *Santa Fe* and we bought our tickets on a sparkling, promising late March day and piled into seats that had a heavy musty smell. I sat with Mother, my stomach fluttering with apprehension and excitement. In the belly of the bus beast was our voluminous luggage—everything that was left of our possessions.

I felt the import of that momentous event, which I sensed would surely remain with me the rest of my life. The brink of adventure! What could be more enticing to a young girl who had heard tales of American pioneers and explorers? I was just like them, I reasoned, except I was traveling east instead of westward.

We rolled out of the terminal—a modest hangar-like structure enveloped in gas fumes and populated with hard-luck figures passing the time by watching buses leave for what they thought were better places—and headed for Bakersfield. I have no recollection of Fresno or Bakersfield except that we passed a lot of gas stations and small hamlets that had just one store and a few houses.

I do recall a growing nausea from the gas fumes that seemed to be directed back into the bus rather into the increasingly vast and open country outside the window. Boredom, fatigue and a sick feeling in my stomach conspired to make me thoroughly miserable just hours into the trip. This was no fun and not very adventurous, I concluded, in dismay.

But then we crossed the Colorado River and headed for Flagstaff and Albuquerque. What a change! The land opened to offer wide vistas of grazing lands, then dessert. All of this was very exotic, fresh and invigorating. The nausea let up briefly while I gazed out the window to take in the cacti and sagebrush that gave a modest, muted green relief to the sandy landscape. This was Indian country for sure and I imagined painted ponies racing across the rock strewn, pebbly terrain.

Instead, I was rewarded with a small group of Native Americans who boarded our bus at a tiny rest stop that was a mere open sided shed somewhere near Albuquerque. Two tattered men and a plump woman with a colorful shawl joined us and seated themselves two rows ahead of us. They had a small baby with them, which was wrapped tightly like a cocoon and was strapped to the woman's back. When she sat down, she transferred the baby to her lap and held it tenderly, facing her. It had dark shiny eyes that disappeared into mere slits as it grew tired.

I was fascinated with the small dark skinned group that looked so different from everyone else with their beaded neck jewelry and colorful pouches. They also carried mundane string bags filled with what appeared to be snacks for the journey and plastic bags stuffed with indeterminable items.

Every American Indian story I had ever heard began to play out before my eyes and I promptly wove my own fable around the little group: They were fleeing the local marshals to put down stakes south of Amarillo.

I had spent considerable time studying a detailed map of the States, which Mother had bought for Manfred and me before we left San Francisco. It was a map that also showed the topography of the country so I knew where all the mountains and rivers were and which ones we were to cross. The map made America come alive for me as a vast and rough terrain, crossed at great risk by early Americans in wagons and on horseback. What valiant, adventurous men and women they were, I thought, and how brave and strong-hearted their faithful horses must have been.

I was deeply moved by the bond I felt certain to have existed between man and horse. To calm myself over the horses' plight, I pictured them at the end of a day of hard travel, drinking peacefully from a clear stream and filling their bellies with sweet summer grass from lush flower-filled meadows. Finally, I had them lie down in the grass, illuminated by a moon crossed by gently drifting clouds. Such were my consolations and they were as fine as a child's dreams can be.

Dozing off periodically, I was awakened only by brief stops on the way to Amarillo and then Shreveport. In Shreveport, I noticed that our Indian passengers were gone and we stepped off the bus for a one-hour rest stop in a dismal station at dusk. The air was heavy with gas fumes and my nausea returned even as we were no longer in motion.

Next we were assailed by the smell of grease on a griddle and cigarette smoke. Mother and I wandered off to a tiny bathroom with a filthy toilet, no toilet paper and a grimy sink. Water had collected at the base of the toilet, a bloated water bug scurried up the soiled wall and a bad smell signaled neglect and germs, especially to Mother.

She produced a bottle of *4711* from her handbag and proceeded to wash my hands with it, which meant rubbing our hands together vigorously as the scent of cologne mingled with that of urine. And that was Shreveport for me.

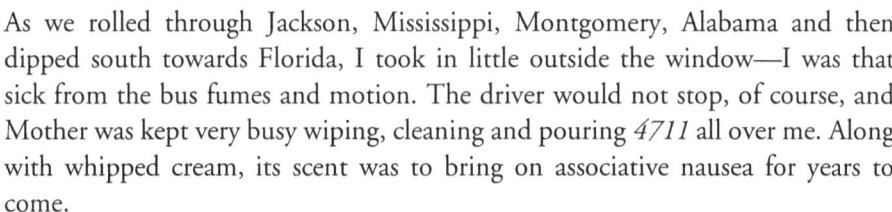

As we rolled through Jackson, Mississippi, Montgomery, Alabama and then dipped south towards Florida, I took in little outside the window—I was that sick from the bus fumes and motion. The driver would not stop, of course, and Mother was kept very busy wiping, cleaning and pouring *4711* all over me. Along with whipped cream, its scent was to bring on associative nausea for years to come.

And it was getting warmer. The bus was not air-conditioned but we were able to open our window, which helped when we were not rolling through polluted towns. I remember reviving somewhat as we saw the first palm trees in Florida's north and groves of citrus trees laden with fruit. They were a welcome distraction from the sorry little towns we had passed through in the days before.

Still, poverty was very evident here in the simple wooden worker shacks with their ubiquitous clotheslines and barefoot children in hardscrabble yards. But their borderline existence seemed less harsh for having been offset by the richness of the dark green grove foliage and the bright sunlight, which cast long shadows from the elegant towering palms. I thought again of Guam and how different that palm-dotted seascape had been. It was a mere two months ago, and yet an eternity in the fullness of the many impressions that had rushed in upon us.

On the fifth day, we finally saw the distant outline of Miami's taller buildings. As we rolled through the outskirts and towards the center of town, the color scheme changed dramatically: We had entered a blue and white city with patches of green and palms lining many of the roads. The buildings were a dazzling white and the sky a cloudless deep blue. As I lowered our window, the scent of flowers was everywhere and even the modest small Spanish-style villas had gardens spilling forth a profusion of colorful blossoms and a tangle of exotic vines. Windows had wooden shutters and flower boxes and roofs were a cheerful red tile. I was enchanted and yearned to leave the bus to explore.

Downtown, where we were headed, was astonishing with its taller buildings and exuberant drivers who favored leaning on their horns. This was no sleepy southern town but rather highly enterprising with fruit vendors on corners, children selling balloons and women hawking baskets in small shady squares.

It was early afternoon and very warm as our bus finally labored into the Terminal and the driver exclaimed wearily, "Folks we have arrived in Miami—end stop. All out, please and thank y'all for riding *Santa Fe.*" With that he stepped off the bus and opened the luggage hold underneath, pushed his cap back from a sweaty brow and lit a small foul-smelling cigar. I retreated and watched as our countless suitcases emerged. I have no idea how we managed to get them all to the harbor that day but miraculously, they were in the ship's Terminal in less than an hour, as were we.

On March 31, 1948 we embarked on our 24-hour crossing to Havana on a cumbersome looking white ferry called *The Florida.* It was comfortingly wide and promised to lie as securely in the sea as a Catamaran might in a lake. But the waters between Florida and Cuba are about as different from a lake as a tornado is from a spring windstorm.

By now Manfred and I were completely resigned to being nauseous in anything that moved and our expectations undoubtedly added to the misery of that full night and day at sea. I remember little of the cramped cabin and hard beds we tried to sleep on and even less of the angry sea outside our tiny porthole. The only time I was on my feet was at the very start of the trip when I stood at the railing, again with Father, and watched Miami's whiteness gradually fade and blend into the sea spray as we churned out into a gray, roiling sea. The wind picked up after the first 2 hours of the journey and tossed sea water onto the wooden deck.

My lesson from the *Buttner* still fresh in my mind, we fled to the pitching, tilting, seeming safety of our cabin where I tried to block out the smells from the kitchen, which signaled a meal of rice and beans in tribute to our destination. I never made an appearance in the dining hall, which was probably poorly attended.

On board were quite a few Cubans or at least Spanish-speaking people, many of whom had brought small packages of their own food for the journey. At the start of our voyage, one saw them in deck chairs munching on sandwiches, bananas and other fruit as though they were facing a certain food embargo on board. Undoubtedly, they only wanted to ensure a repast to their liking.

As the hours passed and we approached Havana, I overheard my parents discussing our entry papers and if they would be accepted.

"What if we can't enter Cuba and cannot return to the States—where do we go then?" I heard Mother say. Immediately I pictured us interminably crossing and re-crossing the tempestuous waters between Miami and Havana until someone might take pity on our plight and allow us to disembark…somewhere.

"We have the right papers from the Americans for Cuba. Do not always think the worst," Father countered impatiently. Turning to Manfred, "Your mother is always afraid. I will deal with these Cubans if they give us any trouble," he pronounced with a discernible swagger in his voice. I felt he needed to discredit Mother so that he could look in charge of our situation or perhaps just make himself feel that way in the event of self-doubt. An early intuition and glimpse of his clay feet awakened in me that day.

We arrived in Havana without incident and were admitted without question.

But no place could have been more foreign to my parents with their roots deep in the pine forests and lakes of Prussia. Here was a sunny, warm land of sugar cane fields and palms surrounded by a turquoise sea of exquisite, shimmering beauty. Moreover, the concept of time must have been banished here for things happened when it was convenient for them to do so—convenient for those calling the shots. It was a life without guarantees or even certainties of the most mundane events.

The butcher had meat when it happened to have come in from the countryside, and stores were open according to when the owner had chosen to have his much-cherished siesta. Mother, despite a fairly flexible nature, was perplexed and agitated over the many uncertainties that each day presented. I was amused and somewhat relieved at the indifference to rules. By contrast, rules still existed at home—Father saw to that—but the contrast between them and the world we now lived in was striking and refreshing. Suddenly a new world order and pace was seen by me to be possible.

We rented a cheerful, bright second floor apartment in *Vedado*, a middle-income suburb of Havana that was also home to the family of a Cuban-American naval officer we had befriended in Tsingtao. It was upon his suggestion that we had even thought to come to Havana.

The neatly whitewashed house had a tiny balcony belonging to our flat, just large enough for two people to sit, shuttered windows and a miniscule front yard with scant growth including a few bedraggled flowers and grotesque-looking cacti. Our kitchen was very plain with a tiny icebox, small black stove and a stone sink that was too deep for me to reach down into. Two small rooms served as bedrooms and an additional room with several tattered easy chairs and a table doubled as a living and dining room.

I loved watching the sun set from our balcony: a stately queen descending in golden robes spread lavishly around her in a blaze of hot tropical light that gave the landscape a celestial radiance. As the grand lady exited, my imagination fired and I was transported to shimmering cities with untold treasures behind the ancient walls of fortresses and *castellos* left behind by the conquistadors. Horses' hooves pounded across fields where ordinary little villas now stood in companionable proximity. Cuba was deeply inspiring and achingly beautiful in its tropical garments of lush greens patterned with a thousand flaming flowers. And all around us was a shimmering sea that changed colors like an eternal kaleidoscope of green-blue hues, dappled by sunlight and molded by wind-frenzied waves.

Even more than in Florida, the air was sweet and heavy with the scent of flowers. I would feel light-headed and intoxicated breathing in its fragrance as we walked with our parents in the cool of the evening across the small green squares bordered by flowers or even when we strolled along *El Prado*, the grand promenade lined with towering palms by the sea. You immediately slowed your pace and moved with the same languor as those around you. Cuba in 1948 was as seductive, even to a child, as ripe mangoes in a sea of sweet, cool cream.

After the first week in Havana, we met the parents of our Tsingtao friend, a friendly, plump couple in their mid-forties—he immaculately dressed in a white short sleeved outfit and she in a white blouse and skirt with ruffles at the hem. Mr. Acosta had a proud, upright posture and his wife a somewhat deferential, shy stance in his presence. They were visibly proud of Cuba and anxious to show us the countryside in their old black sedan with its musty smelling seats and windows that required Herculean strength to raise and lower. Their English was not on a par with Mother's so, with some stumbling about and a lot of hand gestures, we managed to get the drift of what the Acostas were telling us. For once, Father was largely in a listening mode as were the rest of us.

One afternoon, we all drove out towards the eastern end of the island through endless fields of sugar cane. The land was flat and baked hard and dry under a blazing sun; the cane high and motionless in the still air. Between the rows, a lone farmer decked out in a wide brimmed straw hat trimmed the stalks with a vicious looking machete.

We all piled out of the car and walked into the cane fields, Father leading the way. He was curious about this unfamiliar looking crop that supplied the delectable sweetness for which he had an uncompromising weakness. How could these tall dry stalks yield the finely granulated sugar that made fresh blueberries and strawberries a sublime experience, I wondered. But the answer was not available given the limited English of our hosts that day, nor could we muster even one word of Spanish.

That was to change for me very rapidly and in mysterious ways that I can only explain as a kind of language-osmosis that seems to meet less resistance in children than adults.

In the next days, I was enrolled in a coeducational, secular school near our house called *Roston Academy*. A lumbering school bus that had seen better days picked up all the children each morning and deposited us back home in the afternoon.

The teachers were grim disciplinarians, mostly middle-aged women who rarely smiled. If they spoke English, they never let on and all instruction was in Spanish. My first weeks at *Roston* were a blur of bewilderment, anxiety and a deep sense of inadequacy.

In the first hours I was merely gaped at and made to feel as though I had alighted from a distant galaxy but that soon changed. My death sentence was pronounced when the homeroom teacher, more aptly described as a fang-toothed viper oozing venom, identified me as German to the class, adding that I was from that country where Hitler had killed so many innocent people. That put me cheek to jowl with Satan and, in everyone's eyes, gave me ominous, fearsome powers that needed to be stripped in the bud. Cuba's awe-inspiring magic was tarnished for me that day. I was too stunned to cry and too afraid to protest in words I did not yet command.

At recess in the courtyard, I was stormed by a group of girls whose fists rained down on me while they shouted words whose meanings were not hard to guess. I transformed myself into a numb, deaf, stoic pillar of passive resistance. Thankfully, I can remember very little of those first school days except that I was the only child to sit alone while eating my midday sandwich in the shady interior courtyard that rang with the happy chatter of young, conspiratorial boys and girls: a new taste of loneliness and isolation.

One later incident remains with me vividly. Punctuality, cleanliness, and obedience were the law of the landscape at *Roston*. Cleanliness was insured by Mother, obedience was partially observed by me out of self-defense and I made a great effort to arrive punctually at all my classes. To thwart that rule meant public ridicule by the teacher and a severe warning that the next time one was tardy, the fearsome, oversized ruler would be applied to one's backside. In my view, ridicule and humiliation were by far the cruelest punishment. Physical pain would vanish soon enough, I wagered.

So it was virtually inevitable that one day after lunch, when the plan was undoubtedly hatched, three girls stormed me before Spanish class and locked me in a supply closet amidst chalk, stacks of lined notebooks and a great deal of dust. My back was jammed against the door, my face pushed into the mound of stacked chalk. I was terrified and fought a growing panic born of claustrophobia. At first, I was not even concerned with being late for class—that was a minor "inconvenience" despite its inevitable retribution.

I had to get out of there or suffocate on my anxiety. I struggled for breath, then screamed with every fiber of my body, or so it seemed. When I finally heard the rustling of skirts that signaled an approaching "guard" armed with the mighty ruler, I steeled myself for a barrage of abuse in Spanish, which was not that hard to tune out when you don't understand most of the words. And it came as soon as my sour-faced "liberator" turned the key and set me free with a final string of angry words that sailed at me on a dank wind of putrid breath.

There were no questions regarding how I had arrived in the closet. By implication, I had locked myself inside in a move of ingenuity that transferred the key to the outside of the door. As she marched me into class, she delivered a brief speech on the virtues of punctuality and the precious learning time lost when an incident such as this unfortunate one occurred. With that I was banished to face the wall in the far back corner of the room. At least I could not see the smirking faces of my classmates nor be further enraged by the sight of the "pillar of justice" that presided over the room.

I was not new to injustice given my experience with Fey in Tsingtao but I was more deeply wounded and distraught by this incident because I had assumed that in this new world, just off the shores of America, life would be kinder and fairer. At least I fully understood how unjustly I was being treated and never felt for an instant that I was deserving of such discrimination. Instead, I felt a healthy rage that I took home with me and aired in a cathartic rant to my parents. They did their best to explain that there were also many good people everywhere who did not judge individuals by their origins.

"But no one has learned that yet," I protested, "even after all the horrible things that happened in the war."

"It takes time. We are a slow and primitive human race and must still evolve and grow," Father explained. It seemed to me that we were all facing a very long ride to the benign, blinking stars and I saw myself laboring through a black night sky trailing a swath of stardust in a Peter Pan journey that swept me away mercifully from the moment.

I cannot imagine that Manfred fared much better than I at his Catholic, all-boys school, *La Salle*. But I will never know for certain as he buried his pain and shame then as he did later in his life. I realized in the years to come that his experience probably fed a growing lack of self-esteem as witnessed by his increasingly withdrawn, inexpressive nature.

We had fewer conversations than ever and he spent a great deal of time alone, which was not easy to do in our small quarters. Instead, he disappeared for hours, sometimes until dark, and Father would roam the neighboring streets in search of him.

Though we had been growing apart, his absence fed my growing loneliness. He never asked me to join him and none of us ever learned where he went. He simply returned and remained locked down as tightly as a prisoner in solitary confinement. My parents didn't seem to have the energy or insight into his solitariness to try and penetrate his pain. They were too busy being worried about our very existence and uncertain future as stateless citizens with no permanent papers to remain anywhere for long.

Mental health and inner well being were not on the radar screen of most people at that time and Father, in particular, was not given to occupying himself with such "extraneous" matters. His domain was political thought and he was preoccupied with the changing Axis of Power, how Hitler had managed to "kidnap" his country and the future role of Russia and America. Now there were issues!

Three months into our stay in Havana, Manfred contracted a very high fever and lay bathed in perspiration and shuddering in his bed. Next he developed a viciously inflamed throat and had violent nightmares that kept Mother up on many nights. In the day, she hovered around his bed, speaking in soft tones and placing cool packs on his forehead. The doctor diagnosed an advanced case of strep throat and taught her how to inject him with penicillin. That reduced our doctor's bills, an urgent necessity as funds dwindled with no replenishment in sight.

I remember days of hushed voices as we tiptoed around Manfred so he could get enough rest and regain strength. As he got better, Mother transferred him to the balcony during the shady hours so my watching the sunset in solitude was mostly scrapped. The weeks of missed school must have created an additional hardship for him, setting him back in learning Spanish, for one.

While I sensed at the time that Manfred was seriously ill, I only learned much later that he had hovered close to death for several days. In the years to come, he was ill often and I sometimes wonder whether the emotional stress of his teenage years didn't enduringly compromise his immune system. Or perhaps he discovered in illness a surefire way to receive loving attention and escape from the harsh experiences of being a perpetual stranger, even to himself.

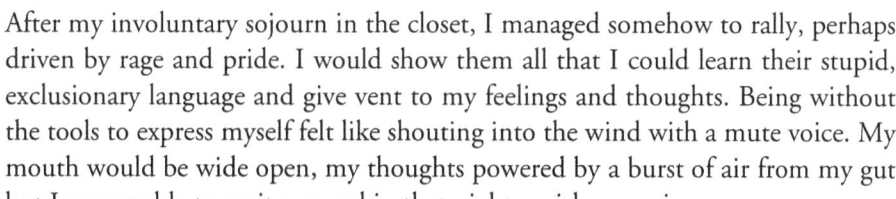

After my involuntary sojourn in the closet, I managed somehow to rally, perhaps driven by rage and pride. I would show them all that I could learn their stupid, exclusionary language and give vent to my feelings and thoughts. Being without the tools to express myself felt like shouting into the wind with a mute voice. My mouth would be wide open, my thoughts powered by a burst of air from my gut but I was unable to emit a sound in that nightmarish scenario.

So, to the exclusion of some of my other subjects, particularly math, I began to memorize Spanish vocabulary words and listen daily to the radio. In the way only children can absorb language, I became increasingly fluent in Spanish and learned to find its sound very pleasing and almost lyrical. Waning was the sense of foreign words catapulted like bullets into an echo chamber. I was mastering their sound and meaning and liking it.

Better yet, my classmates were beginning to actually listen to my fledgling efforts, though, generally, I still suffered more disdain than respect. You don't shed a deeply stained nationality readily and I was making no overt effort to do so, though I never made reference to anything German. That was a mild dodge not a disavowal, I reasoned. I was surviving…painfully but survival was now tolerable. For me that meant a great deal and it went a long way towards building a fragile, tentative self-esteem. After all, not *everyone* survives tolerably, I mused in my sunnier moments.

Father did not concern himself much with my schooling and was also not able to be of any help since he made no effort to learn Spanish. Mother, with only a few words, mostly the names of meats, vegetables, fruit and other staples, puzzled over my books and encouraged me to work hard.

"Soon you will teach me Spanish," she said with visible pleasure. "I cannot get my tongue to handle those sounds but you seem to have an ear for them," she added. That made me proud and served as an additional impetus to attack my lessons and huddle by the old brown radio with the large dials in the evenings.

I came to like the joyful, spirited Cuban dance music with its intricate guitar work, interspersed with shouts of "*Olé*" and spontaneous, rhythmic clapping. I wonder now if I was listening to some of the musical giants from The *Buena Vista Club*…

The summer of 1948 was a hot one, undoubtedly like every other Cuban summer. I leapfrogged from one shady spot on the white-hot streets to the next and awaited the blazing, blood-red sunsets eagerly, as much for their promise of cooler hours as for their dramatic beauty.

And there was always that brilliant turquoise sea with its changing hues on which to feast your eyes and know that you could be in its restoring coolness within a 15-minute bus ride. Yes, the tropics suited me jut fine and I longed to fit in and be accepted. Didn't my growing attachment to the island count for anything, I wondered? Did no one hear the silent songs I sang to its beauty? I began to hope that we might stay.

But, of course, that could not be. Life in Havana was expensive, especially for an unemployed family of four, which had handed over most of its belongings to the Chinese Communists. Still, I heard often that unlike a number of my mother's family, we had not trekked for several hundred miles westward from Poland in a cold winter to save our lives. Her relatives took with them only what they could carry—mostly food. We were momentarily safe though our future was uncertain. And, we were certainly warm, I mused, not without a small ping of guilt echoing in the middle of me.

I often dream in unsettling, provocative metaphors, especially upon rummaging through mind pictures bearing the uncertain contours that over half a century of storage has given them.

A recent dream left me with a familiar feeling of hollow loneliness upon awakening. I was living with my parents and brother in a tall urban apartment building that had long, dimly lit corridors and windows that had no view, giving no clue as to location.

Mother was black, a fact I found unremarkable, and we were poor, equally unremarkable. Manfred, a great deal older than I, was apathetically packing boxes of our belongings to prepare for a move. Father had left us for an undisclosed location with no hint of return and Mother was out doing errands. It was clear that we were preparing to move to a smaller, less expensive apartment with money having grown scarcer. Actually, we had no specific destination; the future was unknown and I felt unsettled and anxious. What lab-tethered scientist proclaimed that dreams are just the manifestation of randomly firing neurons? At the very least, my neurons were not firing randomly.

And so I keep a sporadic Dream Diary to monitor the continuing role of my memories. They announce themselves like ancient tracks of a river carved in dried creek beds; they tell me that nothing lived is ever lost without a trace, and they beckon to be re-examined, maybe even laid to rest.

Autumn in the tropics is a forgotten season. The days don't appear to grow shorter; the temperature doesn't cool perceptibly. But since the days hardly change, one doesn't expect or miss autumn. Havana's skies simply became a deeper, clearer blue and the sea froth blew more frequently over *El Prado* in a fine mist made incandescent by sunlight streaming through the palms.

Then, one afternoon, the winds picked up and bent the top half of the taller palms so that they leaned inland like stately giants striding forward towards shelter. I had just gotten home from school and was foraging for a sweet treat in the kitchen cupboard.

Soon the gusts raised their voices several decibels and became siren-like howls that ebbed and flowed like angry tides. Mother rushed to close the shutters that banged furiously and threatened to leave their hinges. I peered through the slats at a yellowing sky that hurled leaves and dirt through the heavy air. My first hurricane! I was ready for nature's great theater and in awe of its power and fury. How good it felt to be safely indoors. How comforting to feel safe.

For us, the season brought important change. In mid-October we learned that America would grant us a permanent residency in the States. Our little household heaved an almost audible sigh of relief but I began to feel a knot in my gut at the impending loss of yet another home. To be sure, it was a feeling mixed with acute anticipation since I had not forgotten that our ultimate goal was America.

Once again, we were packing, that is, I was watching while Mother did all the work. Father presided with instructions at every turn and Manfred ducked out of the apartment as stealthily as he could. It was far more desirable to remain a child without a sense of responsibility than to join the adult world of woes and worries, we must have reasoned.

There were no dramatic farewells because there was so little we were leaving behind other than the kind Acostas who had given us our early glimpses of Cuba on rare car trips. Manfred and I certainly did not miss school where we had made no friends. But I had at least sharpened my teeth on the hard edges of bigotry and bitten back occasionally. When words failed me, scowls and gestures did the trick. I was filled with contempt, anger and considerable pain and announced to my parents that I wished to become a lawyer one day and defend the defenseless. I was encouraged strongly, particularly by Father. That settled my future, I concluded with certitude and satisfaction.

Again, we boarded *La Florida* or *The Florida*, depending on your embarkation point. This time it was the former, as marked in large letters at the harbor. It was a late October day when a brisk wind swept billowing clouds across a brilliant blue sky and painted cool, dark shadow-patches on the water.

My stomach lurched at the recollection of the stormy passage in the spring and I felt a knot forming deep in my stomach as I steeled myself for the hours at sea. Mother took my hand and managed a nervous, encouraging smile. Father strode purposefully up the gangplank with his lopsided, felt hat pushed far down over his face. It helped to obscure the scowling, determined face he always wore at the imagined prospect of a battle.

Thankfully, there was none. We boarded after a brief check of our papers by the Cuban officials in the departure hall and descended to our bargain-rate cabin below. It was stuffy in our lower realm—close and musty from the damp that permeated the bedding.

Soon we were churning out into a restless sea for the third time in six months. I do not even recall strolling on the deck as we ploughed out of Havana Harbor. A part of me did not want to see the shore grow distant and diminish into a line of haze on the horizon. The time had not been a happy one but the island was still a sparkling emerald in a sea so clear that I had often thought I could see through to the center of the earth where I believed sea beings were born. On that day I felt Cuba slip away and become a memory even before we had left its waters: turning events into instant memories was a way to move forward. But it was still hardly getting easier to let go of places no matter how much I was called to practice.

The voyage to Miami was even more turbulent than the passage to Havana. Late October is not a docile season and a gathering wind whipped up the sea into a frenzy of froth and created deep troughs between giant waves that pounded the weather beaten sides of *La Florida*. I did not arise from my bed until the shores of Florida were in sight. One inadvertent glance in the mirror showed a face that was greenish-yellow and drawn. I tried to focus on a mental image of solid, stable, tranquil land crowned by a steady horizon that held the land in place. My success was limited.

The crossing left me unsteady on my feet and when we finally arrived in Miami, I chose to crawl down the gangway on all fours—a bedraggled creature of wild hair and reluctant limbs. I was sick, dizzy and suddenly irrationally terrified that I'd be left behind an orphan in uncharted land between countries, not granted permission to the one and unable to return to the other. The anxious, frenzied exchanges of my parents over their fear of being turned back at the last moment by the U.S. Immigration Service rang in my ears like frantic sirens announcing calamity.

Mother and Father were sufficiently preoccupied with their worries and apprehension to give much weight to my curious mode of passage after assuring themselves that I was in their midst. Mother, urging me onward with encouraging words about how I would feel better soon on solid ground, was a gentle, preoccupied shepherdess in unsettling, new territory. Manfred strode ahead with Father in a visible effort to assume manly leadership. He was not entirely convincing in his short pants and escaped shirttails that lifted with every breeze.

I fought fiercely with my nausea as the gangway swayed and the fishy smell of putrid harbor water wafted upwards in a vicious assault on my nose. Desperate not to get sick in front of the officious looking immigration officers, I gulped for air and tried to imagine a meadow filled with fragrant, sun-splashed flowers.

And then we were through the gates and past the guards. No one had frisked us or even asked a lot of questions. A friendly, uniformed man leaned down to me after looking at the passport Mother handed him for me and smiled sympathetically. "Not feeling too well, are you? Those are mean waters out there but you're on solid U.S. ground now. Welcome to America, young lady!"

No one had ever called me that before and right then, an uncertain child straightened up to try and become a young girl.

We spent that night in a small hotel near the harbor—all four of us in one room after two cots were installed for Manfred and me. A large wooden fan whirred overhead and particles of dust danced in the shafts of light that came through the half open wooden shutters of our two windows. I silently thanked the walls and floor for remaining solidly steady.

A welcome exhaustion settled over me but we all regained our appetites sufficiently to venture into the downstairs cafeteria and have a meal of toast and eggs.

The simple food tasted delicious and we topped it off with dishes of canned, crushed pineapple—a food that would forever remain quintessentially American for me. But it must be canned to fit the bill.

Louisville Halcyon Years: 1949–1952

Our next destination was wildly incongruous for a German diplomatic family with shaky language skills and rooted deeply in European traditions and tastes. We were off to Louisville, Kentucky, gateway to the South, home of the mighty, flood-prone Ohio River and belching smokestacks from the breweries of the thirties.

Once again, the Acosta family was the tugboat that moved our directionless little family forward in unfamiliar waters. They had suggested in Havana that we move to Louisville as Mr. Acosta had a sister who inexplicably lived there. She was probably the only Cuban in the entire state. Since my parents knew next to nothing about America much less where employment opportunities were most likely to be for Europeans, they girded themselves with optimism for the journey northward.

Perhaps traveling a thousand miles north of the tropics promised a comfortable, more familiar terrain, for Mother found palm trees stark and dull and could not tolerate the heat.

Did they imagine and long for the pines and lakes of northeastern Europe? Did they think that the gentle, southern folk of Louisville would be kinder to former German officials in late 1949 than people further north? My mother can no longer remember her hopes of the time and I cannot piece together their reasoning. Destiny has its own long-range reasoning, often uncovered decades later, or never.

We took up residence on Madelon Court in a tiny rented house in the shadow of the mighty red brick Fehr's Beer Brewery. It was undoubtedly worker housing—efficient, neat and compact with a toy-sized front yard guaranteed to require no upkeep. The houses were all alike and close enough to peer into your neighbor's kitchen sink. Two young poplars graced the block, a recent gesture towards beautification. But nothing could thrive happily in the overpowering stench of the brewery whose stacks puffed as relentlessly as a desperate chain smoker with nothing left to lose.

Mornings were the worst and there was no escape from the stench not even for the unhappy dogs that roamed the streets freely. It was clear that we could not stay there long, especially because Mother was convinced that the air was poisonous. While Tsingtao had a brewery, built by Germans at the turn of the century, it never announced itself to us in that way, perhaps because of the constant fresh breeze from the sea. Fehr's Beer caught us unprepared, while relentlessly readying us for an aversion to beer that was to last decades in my case.

Even during the brief three-month stay in the gray shadow of the brewery, Manfred and I were enrolled in the local school. I was now in fourth grade, though without the benefit of a full command of English, nor the previous curriculum that had brought my classmates to that level.

I recall struggling over daily tests from *Scholastic Magazine* that monitored retention and comprehension. The result was that I was retaining facts that I could not comprehend and recording them in poor penmanship with multiple spelling errors. I was naturally assessed as not being the brightest porch light on the block. Add to that a faint German accent and a visible uncertainty in my demeanor, and I became a natural target for those in need of bullying someone they thought to be lesser than they.

"You're a Nazi—your parents put people in camps where they were treated mean and then killed," one boy shouted while spittle dribbled down his chin. He had red hair and was very thin: the runt of the litter, I reasoned. But it didn't hurt less or feel less unjust for my assessment of him. I stuck out my tongue at him in a weak gesture of defiance and then lapsed into silence the rest of the morning.

Manfred could not have fared better but we knew nothing about his struggles. He continued to keep them locked up as though they were atomic waste buried deep in Nevada's Yucca Mountain. But there they ticked away.

It was a hard time for Father as well. Boredom and loneliness dogged him as he found himself on the small isolated island of his family surrounded by a strange and unfamiliar sea of undistinguished, honest faces. Further, he had great difficulty understanding the lilting southern accent of Louisville's kind and simple folk of the time.

Men ambled off to their nearby work in the mornings, often carrying odd, metal boxes, which he assumed contained tools rather than what turned out later to be lunch. Wives in faded aprons stood in doorways to see them off while small children tugged at their skirts for attention. An urbanized *stetl* in Poland's countryside must have come to mind, devoid of rural charm.

There was no one to invite for dinner with whom to discuss the future of Germany and Europe, then retire to a comfortable drawing room with cigar and cognac while Mother made coffee and lit the tall silver candlesticks we no longer had.

He resorted once again to daily letter writing and entries into a tattered black leather diary in his small, neat script. He used a thick, clumsy looking *Montblanc* fountain pen that had been in his possession since the start of his career in Berlin. It never left whatever makeshift desk he used during our early years in the States and I cannot remember his hands without ink stains.

It did not escape Mother's attention that most letters were addressed to her sister, nor did he bother to make a secret of it. She was expected to accept the unalterable, unfaltering love that he kept alive in his loneliness. To the degree that he wrote, he isolated himself from the rest of us and sunk into long periods of sad silence. He was expertly creating his own darkness while stealing Mother's light.

Occasionally, they argued bitterly and I heard Mother plead with him to leave her sister alone to forge her path and raise a family. But that is precisely what he could not bear: the thought that Freda had a new life without him, new preoccupations and duties outside of his sphere. "I love two women and always will," he shouted angrily as though she had asked something unreasonable—even unheard of. "There is nothing that Freda takes away from you. I have enough love for more than one," he added as though he had a unique, magnanimous gift for passion that she did not properly appreciate.

It is then that Mother would close quietly like a flower at dusk as though to conserve strength for unfurling the next day. She turned to housework and the exploration of the neighborhood, always with an eye to the least expensive produce and meats with which to nourish us. She cooked delicious freshly made soups, richly flavored with her favorite, dill, and roasted inexpensive cuts of meat ringed with seasonal vegetables from a small Kroger's store just two blocks away.

And she baked. Did she ever bake! Not a week went by that she hadn't produced yet another of her fabulous cakes or a tray of cookies, rich with chocolate chips from a recipe for Toll House cookies on the back of the yellow package of chocolate bits.

She made a *Sandtorte,* faintly lemony and rich with butter, strewn with powder sugar and smooth as the finest beach sand on a Caribbean island. Her chocolate cake was decorated with sugared violets and a nut cake was topped with whipped cream and crushed pineapple. Food became a consolation, a balm, a symbol of restored normalcy—a substantive healer of wounds.

We filled out notably at her hand but, miraculously, did not get fat. There was no snacking between meals, no potato chips, no soda, few nuts and certainly no television. Even if we could have afforded such extras, they had not yet permeated our European sensibilities. We were slender, oddly dressed and alone in a society of affable, sociable, well fed southerners who found us as odd as a tailless raccoon or a house with no door mat saying, "Love is a Warm Puppy".

Of course, I wanted desperately to look like my schoolmates, draw my words out lazily and melodically as they did, and be thought of as a normal, often invisible, nice girl whom everyone wanted on their team.

Instead, I was gaped at, teased for my hard-sounding, halting speech, and asked where I bought my funny looking clothes. Mother had sewn them late into the nights without patterns and a sewing machine, which was beyond our means.

She had not forgotten to pack fabrics in China from which she made curtains, tablecloths, napkins and pants for Manfred for years. The fabrics were of excellent quality with beautiful fast colors that never seemed to fade no matter how often she washed them. But they were decidedly different from anything my classmates wore. Moreover, I had just two dresses and one skirt, making me the brunt of much laughter.

"We always know it's you, Vera, when we see that same ol' blue dress of yours," they taunted. "Doesn't your Mama ever take you to Woolworth's?" How I hated my clothes and wished they weren't home sewn! I was ashamed that Mother sat late into the night and sewed instead of buying the colorful, ruffled dresses for me that the other girls wore. I was certain that if my clothes looked American, the other kids would finally like me better.

In the meantime, I did what I could: I practiced drawing out my words and peppering as many sentences with "ya'll" as I could. In no time flat, my English was transformed almost beyond comprehension for my parents. But kids no longer scrambled to avoid sitting next to me and sometimes I was even invited to join in their schoolyard games.

It did not help that I was an awkward, bumbling child—not good at jump rope and only passable at jacks. I was dogged by a fear of failure and ridicule and too proud to show my misery. So I took few chances. If a game was competitive, I often opted out with the excuse that I needed to go to the bathroom or had forgotten a book I needed for homework later.

My teachers were mostly fair and prevented the worst abuses by my classmates but they did not ever offer more help and encouragement than they did to the other children. That was fine with me because it helped me in my efforts to blend in and be less noticeable for my strangeness.

One small problem was my hair. Mother pulled it back from my forehead and twisted it into an odd loose knot on top of my head, festooning it with a large white ribbon that looked and felt ridiculous. The other girls had bangs or pigtails fastened with inconspicuous rubber bands that didn't call attention to their hairdos.

One day in the bathroom, I unfastened the ribbon and my hair tumbled wildly into my face. Being without a comb, there was no way to tame the tangled mess that made me look as though I had just emerged from a night of restless sleep.

My appearance did not escape the homeroom teacher's attention and she reprimanded me in front of the class saying that she liked to see a group of shiny clean faces with neatly combed hair, "not like Vera's this morning." The next day I endured the knot and ribbon but not without telling Mother that I thought it hideous. I wanted bangs, which she found idiotic looking. "You have a pretty forehead," she said. "We must always show our best features, *Kindchen.*" That ended the discussion and did not indicate a possible re-opening in the future.

In those first months I was a sad, lonely girl without really knowing what was missing. I had never had a friend, though I had temporarily invested Manfred with that role when I was around four and before I stopped trusting him, fearing his little malevolent pranks. Friendship was also out of reach at school in Tsing-tao, in Havana and now in Louisville. Looking back, I might have been fortunate in not having had a friend, only to inevitably lose that friend through our many moves. But at that time there was a vague, unrealized joylessness that colored my days. I was getting by without knowing that I could feel so much better.

What I didn't know is that I was on the brink of happiness. After nearly four months in the odoriferous cloud of the brewery, my parents heard of a farmhouse for rent on the far side of town at the outer edge of St. Mathews, a semi-rural section of Louisville, then not yet the suburb it was to become.

The house, a white clapboard structure with a wide, pillared front porch and a stand of tall old oaks, was over a hundred years old and stood on over twenty acres of rich pastureland. A substantial weatherworn red barn and white board fences completed the peaceful Kentucky scene we were about to inhabit.

The day we arrived, several horses, one lone milk cow and a donkey were grazing companionably by the banks of a small stream that meandered through the upper acres. In an instant, I knew from the wild beat of my heart that I had arrived where I was meant to be. It was a knowing that came from a deep place within me, as though I was recalling something lodged in my being that had never made itself known till then.

It was sure and deep but decidedly not of the mind. My new knowing told me that a heart can soar and have no sense of where it is going. It can sing and know nothing of its song. A heart can become a drumbeat and not know it is part of the orchestra. It can fashion a dream not yet dreamt, not yet lived, but still be certain that the dream will be wondrously beautiful for all time.

And so as I stood that early spring day on the edge of a Kentucky pasture, I had knowledge of profound joy to be mine if I held my breath and waited just another minute. It seemed that close at hand: a mere breath away.

Author on Skippy in 1950, Louisville

Author with her beloved cat at the farm, 1951, Louisville

Our new home had two spacious bedrooms and one small bedroom, a glassed in sunroom, a sprawling old fashioned kitchen with a hand ringer for laundry and a large, thick-bodied white refrigerator whose yellowing door squeaked as it opened laboriously on tired hinges.

There was a small dark dining room with a heavy rectangular oak table and a few creaky wooden chairs, hard up against a cluttered living room full of dusty uphol- stered chairs and a worn beige sofa from whose sagging coils and over-stuffed pil- lows it was difficult to arise. But one left its comforting, accommodating softness with reluctance, especially on chilly winter nights when the big black wood-burn- ing stove across from it groaned and hissed out its warmth into the dimly lit room.

My room had a splendid oak four-poster and a generous stone fireplace to the right of the bed. On a tall leggy night table was a dark brown, clunky radio with a round speaker hole covered in worn, dusty fabric. When it didn't sputter nonsen- sical, static gibberish, it offered mostly country music or afternoon soap operas. I remember an endless series of *Lorenzo Jones* episodes in which he had lost his memory. Ask me no more for the rest is lost in a collection of more vivid, edify- ing memories.

I very much enjoyed the music, especially Hank Snow's spirited "Golden Rocket" and Hank Williams' forlorn-sounding blues and high falsetto yodels. The guitar work riveted me and trained my ears to receive and love the work of Josh White, Muddy Waters and others. I still love the slide down a scale that leaves me sens- ing a deep, lonely place I am invited to enter: but, always a place where light can be brought in with just a humble lantern of hope. Oddly, the blues never made me sad, just thoughtful.

Saturday nights brought in *Grand Ol' Opry* clear and clamorous from Nashville and I became a regular listener, sometimes with the radio under the covers, even though I could not abide Minnie Pearl's deafening squeaks and exaggerated slap- stick humor. She seemed to demean my new home and make it a haven of ill- spoken hillbillies while I was working hard on genteel, lilting southern syllables, or so I thought.

The best part of my room was the tall windows that looked out between the porch pillars onto the front pasture with its neat white fence. At night I could see the stars above the smaller oaks and the wandering moon that laid a silver light across my bedcovers.

Only days into our arrival, I noticed a chestnut-colored horse with the fine, veined head of a thoroughbred but a dull coat and ribs that showed prominently. He grazed feverishly on the early spring grass, rarely raising his head and certainly never looking at the eager face in the window that gazed at him on the lucky mornings that he presented himself in the front pasture. An unfamiliar longing tugged at me long before I ever stroked his ragged coat or ran my fingers through his tangled burr-filled mane.

My parents' bedroom had a series of large, drafty windows that looked out onto a neglected vegetable and flower garden and a splendid, sprawling apple tree that produced an astounding crop of deliciously tart apples every autumn. Mother would come to gather the fallen crop and make jars of delectable applesauce spiced with cinnamon that lasted most of the winter and was consumed largely with her crisp potato pancakes.

Beyond our garden with its tall, untamed grass and tumbling, improvisational twig fences, was a cornfield of at least five acres. On windy late autumn days, the dry stalks rustled and bowed their yellowing sheaths towards the rich earth that had nourished them. I cherished their soft murmurings and the waves of paleness that bent to the fresh breezes. Even as nature winterized and readied for restorative sleep, every tree, shrub and blade of grass seemed to me to vibrate with life—with a pledge of birth, regeneration, and fullness. Here on the farm, I embraced the cyclical force of nature with all its hope and promise as I had never done before and it made me giddy for I felt I was finally a part of something grand and enduring.

The more Mother toiled in the weed-infested garden, carried heavy buckets of ashes from the stove into the vegetable garden to enrich the soil, scrubbed the old wooden kitchen floor or prepared tasty meals from limited and simple staples, the more Father retreated to his books and writing desk. Our new world puzzled him with its seeming oblivion to history and strange, contented folk who seemed to live only in the present; he was often silent and appeared to be in a self-imposed exile from which none of us chose to rescue him. A much-needed lull lay over our lives in the first months of rural life.

Still, Father took occasional pleasure in the visible farm population, which included a spirited, vocal rooster and several hens, a growing family of cats that hung around our kitchen door when they weren't hunting mice in the barn, a Shetland pony named Skippy, a ragged chestnut gelding with a noble head, and an old gray plow horse that was "out to pasture" for good.

One day he reported that the rooster had gotten tangled in an old burlap sack and when he had exhausted his own resources to free himself, he trundled over to him for assistance. Father spoke gently to him in German while the rooster stood calmly and tolerated having his legs handled till he was freed.

It was the dinner topic that evening and we all marveled at the wisdom of animals. I was especially riveted by the story, which endeared the rooster to me and slipped him into a small special place in my heart. "Trust is a brave thing," Father said simply of the rooster. I thought about that later in the night as I watched the silver dollars of moonlight slide across my bedroom and tuck into the darkness of the unlit fireplace. I could not think of a time I had been brave in that way.

Manfred, now in high school, was enrolled immediately at the unimaginatively named "Male High" in town and I entered the Henry Clay School in St. Mathews not far from where we lived off Canon Lane next to the Rock Creek Riding Academy. This time I had an easier time of it, having mastered a convincing southern drawl and a solid command of English. I was painfully eager to make friends and to be included in the tittering groups of girls that gathered at recess to share secrets and make girlish plans for after school such as a trip to the local Woolworth's to check out new hair ribbons, decks of cards, paper flowers, rhinestone-studded bracelets and the like.

Progress in the direction of Woolworth was snail-paced, particularly because I had no allowance with which to purchase anything. So, even when I was finally invited once to join two girls on a foray to that wondrous emporium, I made a feeble excuse about fictitious errands I had to run that afternoon, fearing I would be taunted for not being able to buy anything. None of my classmates appeared to come from wealthy families but they did have small allowances that were geared to delicious squandering at the five and dime. Everything there was a treasure as far as a ten-year old in the late forties was concerned.

Still being quite shy and insecure, I leaned towards girls who were not assertive and ostentatious. I noticed Janice early on—her pretty blond hair, her sweet, quietly encouraging smile when I sat next to her quite by chance one day. She was the kind of person who wanted to make you feel comfortable and good about yourself—welcome in her world, accepted with all that might be different and unfamiliar about you yet reserved in the way she opened to you.

"I hope you'll like it here," she said, acknowledging my newness with a shy smile. "The teachers are pretty nice and we do have fun a lot." I was filled with a sense of gratitude for her small kindness that felt as though a wave of warm water had washed over the middle of my chest. I think I managed a tentative smile, at least there was one spreading dead center in the same place where all the warm water was.

I made a permanent claim on the desk next to hers and she made a lasting claim on my grateful heart. During spelling bees, we whispered letters to one another and when the dreaded arithmetic tests were handed out, we shared our tentative knowledge in muted, breathy exchanges. Now, sisters under the skin, we became bonded in ways that we were not yet able to define or even name. But definitions and designations were unessential. We were living an early, fragile, hesitant friendship, my first.

In the darkness of my room at night, I thought about Janice, wondering what I might have to offer up as a token of my gratitude and new, tentative happiness. But I was only at the gate of all the gifts that the little farm was to present and that I might share.

Early on, I befriended Skippy, the Shetland, and climbed daily on his shaggy back, hooking my fingers into his vast mane and prodding him forward with my heels. I hated the idea of kicking him to make him move forward but it soon became apparent that he would merely stand amiably and swat flies with his tail if I did not nudge him with my heels.

I owe a great debt to that brown and white pony whose sweet, patient temperament allowed me to understand and love horses in an enduring and passionate way. On his back, I learned to gently guide a proud, independent being and to understand that only when we deeply become one with animals, are we fully open to the love and joy they offer up so generously.

In the months that followed, I roamed the farm with intense attention to every tree, shrub and clump of dewy ferns that grew beneath the old oaks. And I made them mine. Then there was the extra bonus of tracking the good-natured gray plow horse and the rust-colored chestnut with the fine-boned head of a thoroughbred. I was a Seneca maid looking for the steed that would be her lifelong companion, or a brave in search of adventure and new land to hunt and claim. I lived deeply within the tales I spun of fine and fabulous dreams and poured my overflowing happiness into each new day.

That time of my life was undoubtedly like that of many other children who discover nature in all its kaleidoscopic beauty. I felt an ecstatic union with the life that pulsed around me. It was a profoundly spiritual and totally unselfconscious experience that I knew simply as unbridled joy, which I wanted to hold fast for as long as I possibly could. I knew that it could not be forever as I heard the muted, worried voices of my parents and saw the meager supplies on our kitchen shelves.

Father sought work: a teaching job at the University of Louisville but his interests were too narrow politically to join the History Department, nor did he have any teaching experience. And what learning institution would hire a German diplomat in 1949 unless they wanted to invite vitriolic press coverage or angry demonstrations at their doors?

He finally managed to get an assignment as a guest speaker at the University on the future of Russia for which he received an honorarium of $25. It did cover most of the grocery costs for a month if you avoided luxuries like imported Swiss chocolate. We were grateful to be sure. But it was Mother who decided after the first few months that she must go to work, no matter what the task.

She managed to find two jobs, one sorting and stacking goods in a small stationary business in St. Mathews to which she walked nearly an hour each way. Sometimes on rainy days, the milkman would give her a ride in his truck if he happened to be delivering his bottles on Canon Lane as she trudged to town. They had to shout to make themselves understood above the clatter of the bottles for it was a potholed, unpaved road at the time, more suited to horse traffic.

The other job was close by as a housekeeper for a wealthy lady who was an alcoholic and spent much of the day on her sofa with a bottle on the floor beside her.

Occasionally she and her husband would have dinner guests and my mother would do the cooking as well as waiting on the guests at table and during cocktails. Mother did her job well and cheerfully and was frequently rewarded with sudden hugs that left her employer unsteady on her feet if not actually falling to the floor. These stories left us all sad and, in my case, very perplexed over the lure of a bottle of foul-smelling whiskey. It couldn't have smelled better than the brandy my father used to occasionally have after dinner in China, I reasoned.

The going rate for domestic work was fifty cents an hour but my mother occasionally received a couple of bonus dollars after presiding over parties. On those evenings, she would return home late, having also to do the dishes after bringing the drunken hostess to bed while her husband glossed over her sudden retreat with endless stories from his workday. They could not have been very interesting as his world turned around the Chevrolet car dealership he ran; he was a man of limited imagination and interests but unfailingly kind, as reported by my mother.

Even on gray rainy days when the mud was deep by the barn and the light flat and dull, I harbored a quiet, balanced bliss as I lingered inside the barn and listened to the steady beat of the rain on the roof. I felt safe and whole there, sheltered by weatherworn wood walls and a leaking roof that lent a pleasant damp smell to the hay amply stored in the loft. No place had ever felt so safe before.

One evening when Mother asked anxiously how long we could continue with no adequate income and Father tapped his fingers nervously on the dining room table as he pondered our plight, I said, "those are problems I do not want to think about. I am so happy here that I will leave all those worries to grownups. Besides, we haven't been hungry yet—not like the chestnut whose owner never buys feed for him."

I remember Father smiling at my reasoning and he reached over to stroke my hair. No one yet knew that I was stealing oats from the barrel of one of the other boarded horses to feed Red, the lean chestnut that had awakened my compassion.

On a late spring afternoon with the clouds racing across the sun and dappled light filtering through the first tender leaves in a small grove of birches, I heard the sound of hooves on our driveway. When I walked over to see who it was, I was struck by a dark, slender girl on top of the most beautiful horse I had ever seen. Obviously a show horse, it trotted towards our barn with a gracefully raised tail and a high-stepping gait. The girl seemed to be welded to the animal, totally at one with its movements, her hands low and light on its neck. She held the reins in one hand while the other idled in its nearly white mane. The horse was a deep golden color the likes of which I had never seen.

"Hi, my name's Jeanne…and this is King. I hope you don't mind my comin' over—I was workin' out next door at the Club with King. He belongs to my cousin."

"Not at all," I said eagerly. "That is the prettiest horse I've ever seen and he has such a beautiful gait. Is he boarded over at Rock Creek?" I asked hopefully. This was one horse I wanted to see more of.

Jeanne said that he was but it was dull just riding in their ring. "I really love trail riding. How about you?"

I didn't want to confess that I had not yet been on the many trails in Rock Creek Park, which began right where our fences ended. So I just said that I loved trails as well but didn't have a horse of my own or even one I could take out. She flushed, perhaps afraid that she had embarrassed me with her question.

And then I noticed how pretty and fine-featured she was. Her hair was short and pixie-like and bangs drew you to her warm dark eyes. She seemed a bit older than I and certainly more sophisticated, sitting erectly in a beautiful soft-looking English saddle. Still, there was a sweet shyness about her as a faint color washed over her cheeks when she spoke in her musical southern cadence.

"I'm real glad you came over. Come on and see all the horses in the barn. Most of them are in by now—they get fed around five after the stalls are cleaned." Jeanne dismounted and tied King to an old paint-faded post and we entered the sheltering comfort of weathered wooden walls, soaring support beams and the sweet smell of hay, manure and straw bedding in the stalls. I always felt a rush of pleasure upon stepping through the wide, welcoming door of the old red barn and breathing in the pungent presence of the horses.

We were greeted by the sound of several horses munching their leftover supply of hay, the soft swishing of their tails and the scurrying of cats in search of prey. One cat perched comfortably on the haunches of a placid brown and white quarter horse in contented symbiotic union, or so it appeared.

I introduced Jeanne to each horse by name, giving a brief description much like a proud jeweler might introduce his gems. She seemed interested but, as I was to learn later, her innate sensitivity and politeness may have made her feign interest for my sake. Either way, I liked her almost immediately once I was able to swing my focus from King to her. Such were the priorities of a newly single-minded ten year old who had discovered and learned to love the generous gifts that animals offer up so naturally to their friends.

"If you have a few minutes I'll go out in the pasture and try and bring in my favorite. His owner never stops by to take him in when it's stormy out."

"Why's that? It just doesn't seem right," Jeanne said with a directness she had not yet displayed. "I'll come with you if that's O.K."

It was fine with me, even very welcome, and I headed for the feed room to grab a handful of oats as a lure for Red. "His owner doesn't buy feed for him and rarely comes over so I sometimes take a little feed for him from the other horses' barrels," I confessed needlessly. But somehow it felt good and very possible to tell her.

She gazed at me and I saw a flicker of sympathy in her eyes, a warm look with just a trace of moisture. She placed her hand on my arm and said simply, "I think I know just how you feel. Caring' isn't always spread around equally" and she left it at that.

That is how quickly and naturally we became sisters who were to know each other for life.

As we walked out into the pasture together to bring in Red for the night, the shadows lengthened, the light softened and there was a companionable silence between us until I whistled for the horse, which did not yet know that someone might wish to be its friend.

When you are ten, friendship steals into your life on softly padded feet. You hardly hear it coming and you certainly have not given it a name but you can feel a change in your life. Getting up each morning brings an extra bonus: the certainty that someone will share your joy, your hopes and your sorrows.

Jeanne was back the next day and then again two days later. She always arrived astride King in those first weeks and I suspect she sensed how much pleasure it gave me to hear them clopping down the driveway to the barn where she was always sure to find me. On rainy days, we climbed up into the hayloft, often cradling one of the many kittens in our lap, and talked about horses—what they needed, how smart they were and what good friends they could be.

Our talks were studded with examples, mostly supplied by Jeanne, who had at least a year of experience on me. I listened hard and mused fleetingly about a life that would always include horses.

"You have to be sure they don't get into an orchard and eat too many apples," she advised. "Colic can kill a horse and they're in a lot of pain with it. The only thing that helps is warm bran mash."

"Whoa. I'm glad you said that because I was going to take Red into our backyard where the big apple tree is. I figured he'd get a full meal that way." Now I pictured an agonized horse, lying in the straw of his stall with me casting about for a bran potion that would save him.

My lesson was interrupted by the heavy rumbling of a car pulling up in front of the barn. We scurried down from the loft, our hair full of hay, our noses itching from the dust we stirred as we waded through the piles of hay and clambered down a rickety ladder to the main area of the barn. As we looked out into the soft spring rain and saw steam rising from a nearby pile of manure, a black Hudson pulling a horse trailer had just parked near the barn entrance and a heavy set balding man was unlatching the back of the trailer.

He did not see us nor did we announce ourselves as he led a tall, sleek palomino down the ramp. The horse shook its head vigorously and sent a long white mane flying. It caught the raindrops and the pale light, looking like fine-spun silk tossed to the sky. We were transfixed by the grace and beauty of the animal and only turned our attention to its owner when we heard him speak forcefully to the horse: "Easy, Gaylord. Slowly down the ramp," as though there was no question that the horse would understand his command. And it seemed he did. A swish of the long silver tail, a stomp of a front hoof and Gaylord stood calmly, tethered by a short lead in his master's hand.

Just then the man noticed us. His eyes were a pale, watery blue and they swept over us like searchlights, taking no more time to linger than it takes to illuminate the outlines of objects.

"Hi there," I offered uncertainly. "That sure is a pretty horse."

"He's a champion and about to become very famous. You'll be hearing a lot about Gaylord when I'm through training him".

We were mightily impressed, of course, and asked about his special talents and where we might see him perform.

"This is no ordinary horse. He drives a car and also does arithmetic," he proclaimed, taking in a full lung full of air that expanded an already wide chest. "You'll see him in the circus someday soon."

That is when I noticed his large belly that ballooned out over a belt that fastened baggy pants in a haphazard way that signaled an indifference to his appearance. I had a vague sense of discomfort and so I turned my attention to Gaylord.

Jeanne stood quietly and shifted her weight periodically from one booted foot to the other. She must have pondered, as I did, how a horse could possibly drive a car. To begin with, how would he fit inside? We never thought the man's boast was empty or even improbable. We both just thought that this was yet something else we did not understand in the adult world, which was often so puzzling. Somehow, this was just another inexplicable fact that would soon become clear and wondrous like so much else.

As it turned out, Gaylord *did* drive a car and what a car! The vehicle was a nearly completely dismantled old black clunker whose sides were wooden slats, its roof open with a ramp installed at the rear for entry of any being up to the size of a baby elephant!

The steering wheel was oversized with a knob for a horse's nose to manipulate and there was a large gas and brake pedal, geared to gentle forward motion and soft braking, respectively.

The first time I saw this sizable, bizarre contraption, which received a permanent home next to our barn, I was dumbstruck, awed and amused all in one. Naturally, I wanted to witness a practice run as soon as possible and I was treated to one on a fine early summer day.

Morris Drake, as I shall call him here, Gaylord's owner, was a peculiar person: a bombastic dreamer, a man with a deep love and understanding of horses, a braggart, a man with secret, mysterious desires at least for a pre-teenager, and an unfulfilled fantast. But it took me a while to see all of that. In the meantime, he was a god for owning such a beautiful and talented horse.

We embarked on a fine sunny afternoon with Gaylord at the helm nuzzling the steering wheel, his owner standing next to him and me to the right. There was no windshield so we felt a gentle breeze at our pace of about four miles per hour down one of the roads through Rock Creek Park's golf course.

To say that we stopped traffic is a gross understatement. Cars pulled up next to us, shouted encouragement, took pictures or questioned our sanity. We were seriously in the spotlight and I cannot say that I minded. I was in the pilot's cabin, so to speak, with a genius trainer and a brilliant horse, not quite of this world, I thought. I was where the action was and where stardom was just over the next hill—not even as far as the horizon.

Morrie, as he was known by all, also delighted in giving barn demonstrations of Gaylord's ability to pound out with his hooves the answers to questions like, "What is two plus two?" Almost without fail, he would paw the ground with the correct number of strokes. Naturally, I asked how he had learned to do so but always was told that it was Morrie's great and personal teaching secret that he would never divulge. This made him enticingly mysterious, the keeper of valued secrets, the magician with untold powers. He was a man to be respected and when he instructed me never to handle Gaylord in his absence, except in case there was a barn fire, I listened well.

"Now, *should* there ever be a fire," Morrie instructed, "Gaylord must be saved first. He is the most valuable horse in all of Kentucky and I expect anyone who is here to free him from his stall and tie him up in a safe place." It was clear that we should be prepared to risk our lives. It made sense to me but I knew enough not to tell my parents of the request.

Barn life, as one could aptly call it, was sociable and rife with happy chatter about horses and riding adventures when various owners arrived daily to feed and exercise their horses. There were two brothers, Robert and Miles, both several years older than I who came to care for a quarter horse they owned together and there was another boy two years older than I who owned a black gelding called Ace.

His name was Tommy and he had striking blond hair that often fell over one eye in a way I found fetching and provocative His eyes were the color of cornflowers in late August and his manner was slightly aloof, unavailable, though not arrogant. I suspect he was a bit shy and I found myself watching his quiet way with Ace, the sureness and care in the way he tended him.

I watched to learn and I admired him from a safe distance, always careful that he not feel my eyes on him. I was smitten long before I had even the vaguest notion of infatuation let alone young, hesitant, fledgling love. Not unlike friendship, it crept up behind me until I had to turn and look and give it a name.

In the course of that first summer on the farm, I finally did give it a name. Actually, it was not a *name* I bestowed on this new bewildering, thumping, aching feeling in my chest. It was a mere recognition that I had become like the fragile branches of a birch in the wind when he was near: I bent his way, I leaned into him, I gave in to the force of the gusts that made me shudder in a terrifying delight. And we had not even touched. Indeed, he hardly knew that I was the silent planet circling a sun whose gravity I had bestowed.

By late summer I could stand it no longer and decided that he would only notice me if I asked him to let me mount Ace and take him around our pasture just once. Surely his gaze would be directed towards the horse and if I rode well, he might even gain a positive impression of me. I hoped to merge into Ace and present a picture of graceful unity.

His eyes swung over to me casually and the blue light in them transfixed me into an even more awkward, uncertain figure whose hands grasped each other nervously as though they might flutter off if I didn't hold them tight.

"Sure thing, Vera. He needs a warm up 'cause we're riding out to Big Rock later." My heart leapt. What if the horse was too frisky for me to handle? What if I fell off and he ran away? I took a deep breath and tried to calm my leaping heart, then thanked him in a voice that was just barely steady and audible.

Mounting carefully into the worn, soft western saddle, I laid the reins across Ace's neck to turn him into the lower field of freshly mowed grass smelling as heady and sweet as summer had become for me.

Ace rewarded me with perfect obedience and we galloped off in a steady, controlled rolling rhythm that allowed me to rise and fall easily with his gait, keeping comfortable contact with the saddle. The union between us was so perfect and felt so right and natural that, momentarily, I didn't even wonder if Tommy was watching us. Such was the bliss of that ride along the far fences, the joy at the freedom that we shared with a light summer wind.

I returned reluctantly, mindful of keeping my promise and remaining within the boundaries of an acquaintanceship that I was dreaming fervently into a friendship. I dismounted and thanked Tommy who seemed to gaze at me with surprised and contained approval. Somehow I had placed myself on the outer fringe of his orbit.

But it was to take many months before he held my hand in his, then took me by the shoulders and looked into my eyes and said, "You're real cute and I like the way you handle a horse." I was close to fainting and leaned into him for support without knowing anything about why I needed sustenance.

In the months that followed, there were afternoons when we snuck up the ladder to the loft and lay in the hay, listening to the munching and stomping of the horses below, while we held each other ever so tentatively and tenderly. His hand eventually strayed to my tiny budding breasts and I lived the solace of knowing that I had something that pleased him. I also felt the early stirrings of desire for something I couldn't begin to define. I was now an earnest, enquiring eleven year old, not precocious, just exposed and vulnerable and filled with questions I had no one to ask.

I did not even share the experience of my afternoons in the hayloft with Jeanne, feeling that somehow it was too personal, too intimate and too forbidden to risk disclosing. Besides, there was no initial need to do so even though she had become my trusted and closest friend.

It was not long until her parents bought her a horse—a sweet-natured, bay quarter horse named Lady. Jeanne promptly switched to a western saddle and bridle and rode beautiful quarter eight figures in our front pasture, merely laying the reins over Lady's neck and leaning her body gracefully to one side and the other to guide the mare. No one handled a horse as facilely and effortlessly as she did and I was filled with admiration, awe and a burning desire to become as accomplished as she.

Meanwhile, I had quietly graduated from just admiring Red in the pasture, stealing feed for him and cleaning out his stall to grooming him and swiping carrots from our frig as special treats. The inevitable next step was that I ask his owner if I could also exercise him. Mark Risdale, who might have been in his early twenties at the time and had clearly lost interest in Red, gave his permission readily after a few words of warning about the horse's spirited nature.

"Never let him get the bit between his teeth or he'll be in Lexington before you know it…and you might not be with him," he added with a good-natured wink. I was close to rapture over his trust in me and what I saw as generosity that I had to clench my teeth and pinch my blue-jeaned leg not to lose my composure and break into a loud whoop of joy. I was determined to seem "cool" and grown-up—worthy of handling his horse.

That happy event ushered in countless horseback adventures with Jeanne as we galloped alongside the golf course at Rock Creek Park, descended down to the wide stream that ran through its midst and sat astride our horses as they waded and then swam to the deep pool of water below a giant rock from which kids dived into the water off Big Rock, as it was known to all. Even when the temperature soared to 100 degrees on many summer days, we were cool in our drenched jeans atop our refreshed horses. They drank deeply and thanked us with happy snorts and playful pawing. I often rode bareback, relishing the feeling of Red's muscles beneath me, the power and majesty of his sleek and glistening body.

No matter what the season, we managed to ride together several times each week after school and sometimes late enough to see the moon rise over the tall oaks by the stream. On still, chill autumn nights, we would sometimes lie forward over our horses' necks, arms encircling them for mutual warmth and deeper companionship. Neither of us would speak for fear of breaking the spell within which we lived for we both knew that it was a very precious and perfect time in our lives: a pinnacle on which we stood, requiring that we hold our breaths so that the delicate balance we maintained at this new altitude would not be disturbed.

But the time had come to breathe again, to allow events to take their course and, with it, a turn in fortune. I think it began the day Morrie promised me a starring role with Gaylord in the circus. I was to ride him without saddle and bridle and guide him only with the shifting weight of my body through an elaborate pattern of figures, his white mane sweeping my face and catching the bright circus lights. I would become beautiful as I merged with Gaylord. That was the promise, word for word.

"You will be a star, I know it, and Gaylord will make it all happen. He is a magic horse." Morrie would not be the driving force. The horse would, or so he promised.

That very day we began a daily, rigorous training course during which I rode Gaylord, bareback and without a bridle and learned to move him from a walk to a trot to a canter to a controlled gallop. I was proud, ambitious and just a bit insecure over everything I had to master. Morrie was firmly in control while I was certain that his horse was solely in charge.

But I was certainly not in command the day Morrie cornered me in the tack room and mumbled something about my "pretty little tits".

I had no idea what he was talking about but I could not disregard the way he pressed himself against me with a hard, mean bulge in his middle that pushed against my stomach.

I knew nothing about sex except what horses did to have foals so I was reduced to instinctual responses, which simply told me to free myself from his grasp. But they also told me to do so without jeopardizing my circus career with Gaylord: an early attempt at bartering or trading off.

I feel the heat of shame rise to my face today as I recall my whispered, uncertain protestations and how I did not withdraw my hand when he placed it on his suddenly exposed penis. I did not dare look down as I endured Morrie's hot breath against my ear and as my hand was guided across a long, smooth surface more forbidden and menacing than anything a child is able to imagine. But children know without understanding; are guilty without knowing why; and burn with shame before any prior experience of humiliation.

"Don't, please. I don't like this," I managed, hoping that he would be merciful and return himself to his trousers without being angry with me.

"It's alright. A very natural thing we are doing. You'll learn more about it soon when you're older," he promised in a hoarse, deep voice that was hardly short of a threat by the time it reached my frantic brain.

I pulled back and moved to take down Red's saddle in a shaky effort to change the mood and extricate myself.

"I promised I'd saddle soap it...it's real dry and the leather is cracking. I don't think Mark wants to buy a new one since he's not even buying feed," I prattled on nervously.

Morrie let out a deep sigh and trailed his hand aimlessly across my back. A cold shiver shot down my spine and I wheeled around to leave the tack room, my legs wobbling uncertainly, sweat building under my hairline and trickling slowly down my neck. I was hot and cold, damp and dry-mouthed, angry and afraid.

Neither of us mentioned the incident over the next days...but it occurred again and again and again. Almost always it happened in the tack room, which became a fearsome place when he was around. Naturally, I made sure I was at the far end of the barn, not near enclosed spaces when he showed up but he was crafty and knew that his leverage lay in Gaylord's future at the circus with me and my belief in that future. Asking me to get him a bridle, or a blanket or Gaylord's curry comb, I would head for the tack room with knees as unsteady as willow branches in a windstorm while listening with dread for his inevitable swift steps behind me.

Of course he chose times when we were all alone in the barn, picking odd hours for his appearances. He varied his arrival just enough to keep me off guard and unable to predict when his old black Hudson would pull up beside the front pasture by the barn.

Then, guessing that I was changing my schedule as well, he began parking behind a large old shed out of sight of the barn and then sneaking up on me from the cornfield, which afforded him a clear view of the areas I frequented. It was never hard to find me once he had located Red for the horse began to trail me in the fields. There was always a carrot or a sugar cube in my pocket for him.

But I was still riding Gaylord and learning to show off his gaits without the aid of a saddle or bridle. And I was strictly forbidden to grasp his mane even if I felt myself falling. That was so that not even one hair would be lost of his magnificent silver mane. Morrie made it sound as though a handful of mane grabbed in distress would reduce the horse to hideous baldness, while I would only suffer a few bruises if I fell. Though I found his arguments extreme, I concurred silently and made every effort to keep my hands loosely by my side as I rode.

There was one notable exception the day Gaylord and I headed for a barbed wire fence that I knew the horse could not see. Without a moment's hesitation, I grabbed his mane and swung off in a dead gallop, as much to save Gaylord from vicious tears to his chest as to rescue myself from certain injury.

Morrie ran over to me and without a word of inquiry about my injuries, which were luckily minor, shouted at me. "I told you never to grab hold of his mane, no matter what. Now you have torn out at least ten hairs. No horse has a mane like Gaylord…"

I was dumbstruck over his indifference to my bruised body and felt a healthy anger well up and demand to be heard.

"You don't care about anyone but this horse. I could have gotten killed and so could Gaylord. This is just stupid!"

"Dumb stubborn German girl. You don't listen. Germans never do. That's why you lost the war!"

It was not an identity connection I would have made and it rolled off me easily without leaving a trace. I had heard worse and Morrie's views had ceased to count the day he unbuttoned his fly and unleashed his demon, making it mine as well together with an ever-present, searing shame.

Still, there were glorious days on which I never once thought of being German. As a matter of fact, I began to think of myself in the past tense: I *used* to be German, foreign and a misfit. Now I was mercifully simpler: A young girl with friends who wore faded jeans like everyone else. I liked not being noticed, which made Morrie's attentions all the more painful. They were a regression for me on every level.

I also felt that I finally had something to offer: the wonderful farm on which I lived. Towards the end of our first summer there, I invited Janice to come over and meet my new barn friends, which were the horses as much as Jeanne, Tommy, Robert and Miles. She seemed to be pleased and her pretty blond mother drove her over on more than one occasion.

Since she seemed to want to learn how to ride, I began a gentle introduction to horses, the way I thought was meaningful. First I simply spoke about horses—how they had needs that were as important as ours, and how I always tried to sense what they might be feeling or needing.

She might have been a bit impatient with me at the start, wanting merely to sit astride Red and race like the wind. But she indulged me generously and I thanked her with initial lessons on a lunging line and a swift graduation to riding double with me guiding her hands and knees from behind.

There were sweet late summer days when we cooled ourselves in Rock Creek and ambled along leisurely on Red in the shade of the large old oaks that dotted the park. I can still hear the interminable chirping of millions of katydids and see the soft light of evening send long shadows over the fields that stretched for miles and turned into gentle hills with intimate views into hollows and groves of poplars and birches.

And in between there was always Morrie with his mysterious and nefarious needs, trailing me with his eyes while mine furtively followed Tommy.

"Now you be a sweet girl and meet me in the tack room," he would whisper as he passed me in open safety. "You know that I can't let you ever ride Gaylord again if you don't do Papa that little favor. You'll like it real well when I get through teaching you what every young lady learns sometime," he promised with a hideous smile that I was not yet able to identify as a lascivious leer. It was just different from all the smiles I had ever seen.

Once more I complied and endured the urgent groping that always culminated in trapping my hand on his swollen penis. His enjoyment was evident from the grotesque moaning and heavy breathing that reduced him to a ludicrous and hideous figure I had come to fear and revile. It had to stop and it did.

"I am not doing this anymore," I said with a trembling voice that fought to sound resolute. "And if you ask me again, I will tell Father," not that I had the slightest intention of confessing what I sensed were highly aberrant and certainly deeply shameful activities. I felt as though I had been dunked in a swamp of stinking, moldering matter and covered with pungent slime. There was no longer any choice but to end my enslavement and, mercifully, I had hit upon an effective weapon. Morrie and Gaylord departed for good only days later.

Thirty years were to pass before I could finally speak of that time. It was Jeanne I told only to learn that he had forced himself on her as well. Though it was hardly possible for our bond to become yet stronger, on the day I told her, I felt it did as we held each other for long minutes and wished we had shared our silent shame sooner.

As we rounded out our second year on the farm, Father's restlessness, boredom and agitation over our financial situation reached new levels of frustration for us all. He had become, short-tempered, demanding and a severe disciplinarian, the latter targeting me almost exclusively.

All the while, I had become more willful and confident in my ability to express myself and my needs. I wanted only to be with the horses and my new friends, not indoors doing housework while Mother was at work. It never occurred to him that he or Manfred might also help with the chores. Those were girls' duties in his universe. I was called in from the barn with regularity to set the table for dinner, dust the house, water the houseplants in the sunroom and wash the kitchen floor before Mother came home.

Usually he had to bellow out for me several times before I responded with anything more than a promising, "Coming!" One day he had called for me three times and when I still could not tear myself away from mucking out Red's stall while trying to impress Tommy with my pitchfork-strength, Father stormed into the barn and pulled me out literally by my hair, shouting loudly in German, "*Jetzt wirst Du endlich gehorchen,*" (Now you will finally obey.)

Obey was the operative word in his child rearing manual and a loud decibel strength was the hallmark of his commands. These occasional displays of Napoleonic bravado cast him in a fearsome light amongst all who witnessed his parental efforts.

I was deeply ashamed of him and also angry because, once again, I was reduced to being a person from the country where force and authoritarianism had been ruinous and deadly. My new friends were reminded of my roots and, while I had now graduated to being pitied rather than hated, I felt I was once again an immigrant from a country that had given the world Hitler. If I had one guess to make, I'd say that Tommy, for one, saw my father as a mildly watered down version of Hitler. It did not help give him the courage to lean towards me openly, especially because he had seen Father with his hunting rifle, shooting birds that nested in the large oak by our front porch.

Another time, my open defiance of his calls from the back door enraged him so much that he unfastened his belt when I was finally in the house and beat me across the back with the buckle until I had red, angry welts and one open wound.

My rage at him was white hot and blind. "You are a brute and will pay for this," I screamed at him for all to hear while fighting not to shed a tear. He was to have no satisfaction from his deed and Mother was to hear about it the moment she stepped through the door.

The satisfaction was entirely mine as she gently tended to my back, then turned on Father and told him that such brutality would never happen again as long as she was part of this family. The threat was thinly veiled and gave me an opportunity for a last shot: "I will never forget this day, you can be sure of that!"

Meekness was not in his nature and that day was no different from any other. The house shuddered as he thundered. But the incident bought me at least two months of no corporeal punishment for Mother had stood her ground.

Looking back, it seems odd that, at first glance, such remarkable events come and go as though moving like innocent clouds across an indifferent, silent sky. And yet, though time binds most wounds, the events leave behind a blood mark. Mercifully, it fades with hard-won forgiveness.

There was some respite from Father when he boarded buses to seek out Germans he knew in distant places like St. Louis. He was usually gone nearly a full week.

One such trip yielded a job offer from Anheuser Busch as a night watchman. His friend there, in an executive position, was apologetic but firm in explaining that Father's qualifications were not suited for the beer brewing business. While the truth of that assertion was impossible to dispute, Father still expected, I think, that exceptions would be made for him. Elitism dies hard.

When he returned, he retreated to the simple oak table he had made his desk and wrote. None of us ever probed his efforts but, in retrospect, it is safe to assume that he wrote regularly to Aunt Freda as he had for years. The airmail envelopes from Germany that arrived with regularity attested to that probability.

Mother no longer paid much attention to these distant threats. She was simply too busy fulfilling the daily, basic needs that ruled our lives. There was rent to pay, food to buy and clothes to mend or replace. There were gardens in the back that Mother had promised to tend, wood to be gathered for the stove, apples to be gathered in the early fall, new kittens to feed.

Manfred's activities during that time remain nebulous. He simply did not stand out with any particular passions or even hobbies, other than to occasionally join Father in shooting at either bees or birds, the former when there were no other available targets. Their endeavors were strictly a matter of excelling at a sport and, perhaps, competing with one another.

The targets were just that—seen as inanimate objects that were sufficiently elusive to be challenging to a rifleman and hunter at heart. I made certain to never witness these activities, much less to examine or even glance at the spoils. My life revolved around what pulsed and lived vibrantly and exuberantly at the very moment I was in. Never again have I achieved such a near-Buddha mind and it is not for want of effort. Could it be that children naturally live closer to Spirit and that we stray from our center as the world becomes more with us?

Mother was frantic at the sound of their guns, fearing that we would be chastised or even evicted for dangerous activities that should have been reserved, if at all, for remote wilderness areas.

"Stop immediately," I heard her shout at Father one day. "You are endangering our very existence here. Don't forget, we Germans are only reluctantly tolerated here to begin with…without your shooting calling attention to us!" Too much worry over the years had finally gotten to her.

Father laughed at her mockingly and announced that our mother was being her usual nervous, fluttering self. I distinctly remember the word, "fluttering," which served to effectively undermine her authority with us even though, I, for one, was quietly appalled by anyone taking aim at either bees or birds.

But I was equally distressed by Mother's frequent admonishments that we were merely *guests* in America and tentative ones at that. The very implication of having to leave for yet another unfamiliar destination was simply not something I wanted to deal with.

In my mind, I was now *almost* American, accepted by most of my peers and wearing T-shirts and jeans. The right emblems are important to one who had looked different for so long: In China I had looked western; in Cuba, German; and in America, during the first months, I looked plain foreign and needy, if not straddling the poverty line in my two-outfit, unstylish, obviously homemade wardrobe. Homemade in my world of the time did not convey something that was finely and lovingly crafted, as in the case of my attire. Here Woolworth was King.

Except for school, I was always in jeans, exchanging T-shirts for checked flannel shirts in the winter. They were durable and cheerful, not to mention inexpensively available at Woolworth's. As an added bonus, my farm outfits were wonderful equalizers: We all wore more or less the same thing and, the more worn your boots were, the more you were seen as a rider of regularity—a dedicated horseperson with "working boots".

It also helped to know the words to Hank Williams's hits and if you could also play the guitar, you had star quality. I did *not* play the guitar but it didn't matter since, just having graduated from foreign freak to accepted stranger, was a step forward to savor. And I did.

School had finally ceased to be a problem for me since I now understood everything perfectly and could read English as fluently as the better students in my class. By the same token, I didn't have much interest in my studies, did my homework grudgingly and often carelessly, spending most waking moments thinking about Red, Ace, Tommy, Janice, Jeanne and my new buddy, Lorda, a black kitten that had adopted me.

I have no idea how I came up with that name for such a delicate, shy cat that learned only slowly about the warmth and comfort of my lap. I think I liked the sound as it tripped off the front of my tongue. I had become very fascinated with word sounds—perhaps having had to acquire three languages in my short life—and would often make up words with a foreign sound and faux Latin grammar. The sound of Manfred's tutorials with Father were obviously still ringing in my ears.

At any rate, I loved having a secret language that I felt no one but Lorda, Red and I could understand. We were thus conspirators and members of our own exclusive society of three. I would whisper to Lorda, "*Meus catus istus bella*" and hold her to my cheek till she squirmed out of my grasp and settled nearby to scrutinize her puzzling mistress with eyes that were golden globes like no cat's I have seen since.

Tantalized by the rhythm and tone of my words, I would cast about for new phrases whose music captivated me while neglecting to make much sense. "*Amore de flores est grande in summer,*" I would sing out to Red, embellishing the words with a small tune as accompaniment and repeating this "chorus" till the horse pawed the earth and threw his head high in what I interpreted as appreciation of my incantations. My world was full of magic in those days, making anything possible if dreamed with sincerity and longing.

On crisp fall days I would trudge through the fallen leaves, trying to walk silently like a young squaw. I was creeping up on an enemy camp to view their horses and decide if there was one worth rustling; or I was following the trail of a deer to discover where it lived and if there were fawns born before the winter cold. Perhaps I could rescue them and put them in the barn with their mother till the spring came. The implausibility of such plans never deterred me when I walked on the wild side of reality, the terrain of endless possibilities.

On frosty winter days, and when there was an infrequent snowfall, I headed for the barn's warmth and the musty, sweet smell of hay, hoping that Tommy or Jeanne would be there to trade news of the day. One thing we never talked about was school. One would have thought we were perpetual truants, country bums with straw in our hair and Hank William tunes on the brain.

But I had discovered books, though I never mentioned my new interest. There was "My Friend Flicka," "Black Beauty" and the tales of Zane Grey and Jack

London to read with a flashlight under the covers at night. House rules were that I be in bed by nine with the lights out, an impossible edict for me when there were such heart-tugging and imagination-firing stories to devour, ones that gave me new material for my world of magic.

My parents certainly did not discourage reading but Mother placed the need for sleep above that of firing the imagination, at least until I was in my early teens. She was ever practical, never the dreamer and I knew even then that we did not need yet another dreamer. Father lived in a former century and I clung to a present vividly embellished by my imagination. While he spoke of the Kaiser's time and the noble, privileged landowners whom he saw as having set a high standard of ethics for Germany (only temporarily breached by Hitler and his thugs), I spoke with the trees, horses and cats that roamed my Eden and all knew that we were in the perfect garden.

It has taken decades for me to remember that you can craft your world with your dreams.

And as our third year on the farm brought autumn once again, our plight caught the attention of our local minister, a young man in his mid to late twenties. We attended church with some regularity but I cannot say I was an enthusiastic attendee.

For one, I felt embarrassed every time the collection plate was passed down our aisle and Father would deposit a few coins in a plate brimming with bills. He did not believe in tithing and was not averse to announcing his view that the Church had robbed its parishioners for centuries to line its own pockets. Fortunately, such declarations, while sometimes made in church, were always made in German and presumably not understood by anyone. Still, I reddened and cringed for his strong voice alone called disapproving attention to our little group. Mother was equally mortified and hissed at him to stop, usually to no avail.

Sunday mornings in church were also a waste of precious time in my view. I was missing the opportunity to gallop through the park, tussle in the hay with Tommy, or plot ways to steal grain for Red's dinner.

That is not to say that I didn't have conversations with God. Only it wasn't anyone I called "God" but a spirit that knew that I existed, cared and listened to my hopes. Someone benevolent was always walking alongside of me and I thanked him for it with simple words and hands that didn't meet to announce those private conversations.

But much changed on our last Thanksgiving Day in Louisville. The previous Sunday at church we had heard our minister announce that there was a needy family in the congregation, which might not be celebrating Thanksgiving with a turkey dinner the way most everyone else would. He announced a special collection for their meal and asked us all to open our hearts. I listened and wondered of whom he might be speaking, blushing at the thought of Father's habitual miserliness when the plate was passed.

While I knew of no plans for a turkey dinner at our house on the upcoming holiday, I felt a pang of pity for the unfortunate family that was probably foreign and could perhaps afford even less than we.

On Thanksgiving morning, Mother was busy in the kitchen marinating an inexpensive cut of beef for what was to become Sauerbraten for dinner. She was apologizing for not having begun marinating the previous evening, which she needn't have done. We all knew she had returned home late from her housekeeping job and fallen into bed exhausted. We reassured her that it would be delicious and tender nonetheless and certainly ample from the looks of it.

I scampered off to the barn after breakfast and tended to Red, grabbing an extra helping of oats from one of the other horses' bins before anyone arrived to witness my stealthy misdeed. He was to commemorate the day with a good meal like the rest of us. It was only just and appropriate, I reasoned without the slightest twinge of guilt. A righteous deed always justified its means in my book.

Then I heard the rumble of a car, a large wood-paneled station wagon that pulled up on the side of our house by the kitchen door. I looked over uncertainly and then registered considerable surprise since we rarely had visitors. As the driver's door opened and a pair of long legs emerged, followed by the familiar tall, slightly stooped frame of our minister, a sickening surge of fear coursed through my gut. No doubt he had heard of my stealing and had come to speak to me and, worse yet, Father, about it. This would be no day of giving thanks for me, I concluded.

To my further surprise, he walked to the back of the wagon, opened the door and proceeded to carry the first of two sizable cartons to the kitchen steps. A closer, tentative look told me that they contained groceries and with a rush of sweet relief I recalled his words about the needy family on the previous Sunday. Close on the heels of my relief came an unsettling mix of embarrassment and gratitude, followed by a small ache in my chest and the sting of willfully harnessed tears. I knew that I would find no words to utter for his kindness. So I stayed put for the moment.

Mother was visibly overwhelmed by such a spirit of giving. Father was reduced to stammering heartfelt thanks in his heavy German accent. "You are so kind. We know not how to thank you enough." And then in a spasm of pride he added, "We are doing well here in your wonderful country and on this nice farm. The children love it and we are very grateful to America…and you. You needed not to do this…"

The minister understood perfectly. He bowed graciously in a formal, overly respectful way as would not have been customary for him with any of the other parishioners. He must have felt that Europeans required a different stance, obviously displaying considerable sensitivity.

If events can be tenderly memorable, that one remains as shiningly unforgettable as a first kiss on a June night ablaze with fireflies. For me, it endures as well for its proof that a spirit of love hovered around us, beckoning that we recognize it and give thanks. God didn't just hang out amidst church pews, I concluded.

In the evenings, there was now increased talk of change. Mother said we could not continue living "on the edge," scrambling to put enough food on the table and pay the modest rent on the drafty farmhouse we called home.

I felt a growing knot in my stomach for the inevitable departure I sensed on our horizon. Still, I fought not to think about it and did not even voice my fears to Jeanne. But at night I would slip under the covers with Lorda curled up against me and tell her of my secret terrors. Clearly, we would have to leave the remote farm life and travel to a city where Father could find work. There would be no animals there, no birches bending in the wind, no timothy hay sweetness in the air. But till then, I was going to live yet more fully and completely in the moment than I had ever imagined possible.

During our last autumn in Louisville, I took to wandering through the woods on the property's edge and collected bright fall leaves, which I pressed between the pages of my favorite books. When the day came to leave, I would have a thousand reminders to color my memories. It was a time that must never fade, I vowed.

And when Red shed a shoe that winter while trotting across an icy patch, I stopped to pick it up and save it for all time. That day I promised myself that I would never forget him and our bond would stay intact over how ever many miles might separate us. I was as certain then of our timeless connection as I am today that the sun will climb steadily in the east every day until the end of time.

In early December, Father traveled to New York to accept a position in the German Consulate as head of the Passport Division, including the department that arranged compensation for Jews who had survived Hitler.

My parents were visibly buoyed by their good fortune and so anxious to begin our new life in New York that Father stayed on immediately and sought an apartment for us with plans that we follow him in January. It left Mother with all the packing.

I was useless, having fallen into the first depression of my life that left me so despondent that I could hardly arise in the morning, could not sleep at night and forgot to eat unless prodded. I could not even weep openly and with abandon. Instead, the tears trickled quietly and steadily down my cheeks.

I carried Lorda around everywhere with me, much to her frustration and begged Mother to let me take her to New York.

Mother cannot have known how much Lorda's company would have meant to me when she answered impatiently and distractedly that pets were not allowed in the building where we were to live in the Riverdale section of the Bronx. She did not invite a further discussion of the matter, turning to the suitcases that were lying open all over the house.

I stormed and raged at her as I had never before done but she turned me away with short answers that scarcely acknowledged my distress. She was mightily preoccupied with embarking on our new road and my childish needs, as she saw them, had to take a back seat.

There was somehow no room for those needs, which I can only attribute to her lifelong indifference to animals. While she would never have harmed any living being, she also had no space in her heart for animals and could not understand their meaningfulness to others. She herself had grown up totally without pets, undoubtedly because of the dirt and disorder they were said to create. Cleanliness was King in the Prussia of her childhood: a bleak, pristinely ordered world in my enduring view.

Even more devastating was taking leave of the best and closest friend I had ever had. Jeanne had shown me the joy of sharing experiences and even some secrets. She understood my love for animals, my love for the land and its changing reflection in the regular roll of the seasons.

She was tender and quietly soothing when I was desolate over the death of a kitten—not uncommon since rat poison was routinely placed in the barn by cautious horse boarders. She was steadfast in her comfort and support of me when Father raved and reached for his belt over trivial transgressions of mine. "I'm sure he doesn't mean it," she would say softly, as much at a loss for explanations as I was. He was fundamentally foreign to all of us and it made him a lonely, cranky man.

Fortunately, Tommy and I had drifted apart over the last year on the farm. I think that Father terrified him and perhaps he harbored the forbidden fantasies of all young boys, making him guilty before he had lifted a hand to make good on them. Better to stay away from trouble, he might have reasoned.

I, too, lost interest, particularly after Morrie had shown me what lurked in his trousers. I was not ready or prepared for a snake in the grass, as I had begun to see male equipment, when horses were without guile, simple and straightforward. I always felt rewarded by them for my affection. Tommy had floundered too long among my budding breasts and been too impatient with my reticence.

Jeanne came to the farm daily in the weeks before we left and we held hands and cried together, promising friendship for life. And we kept that promise though I was never again to live in Kentucky nor was she after her mid-twenties. Ohio claimed her thereafter.

I will not dwell further on those last weeks on the farm for even today their memory leaves a dull ache in my chest. I will say only that I handed an unsuspecting, somewhat bewildered Lorda over to Jeanne the day before we boarded a train bound for New York and that I wept into the palms I held to my face most of the way north. In a brown pouch handbag, I carried Red's shoe and a fistful of straw from his stall. I would not look out the window to witness the miles left behind. All else remains a fuzzy smudge of charcoal across a steely blue January sky.

New York, A Rocky Road

It is hard today to re-imagine how much I reviled New York in our first year there. Everything that is vital, stimulating, exciting and promising about that city was as lost on me and as foreign as a tropical rainforest might be to an Eskimo.

We moved into a six-story apartment building overlooking the Hudson River on a street in the Bronx with a funny name, Kappock Street. It had a small terrace that felt like a lonely island in a lifeless sea-sky and, never having been fond of heights, looking down from this penned-in space made me dizzy and mildly nauseous. I wasn't to witness much light in those early New York days even when a glorious sunset turned the Hudson's waters to gold.

The joylessness that enveloped me in a gray shroud clung to me month after month. I had no name for it nor did I need one. It just *was*, like rain when you long for sunny vistas, like mist when you dream of sweeping, crystal clear views.

Nothing could have been further removed from the open-spaced freedom of the farm than Kappock Street. I was paralyzed with despair and longing for everything left behind. There was no way out as far as I could see and I soon even stopped asking when I could leave New York for a visit to Louisville.

"You must learn to adjust, to be flexible," Mother advised. "Life requires that of all of us," sage advice but unheard by a twelve-year old in misery.

Not only was adjustment as foreign to me in those days as yak butter would be to a diner at *Tour d'Argent* in Paris, but I was filled with enough fury to detonate a nuclear weapon.

My anger was palpable to everyone around me and I made no effort at gentility, especially not around my parents. My family was meant to suffer for my exile and misery. There had to be *someone* responsible for the pain that burned within me with a thousand leaping tongues of fire.

"I hate you both and hope you will burn in hell for this," I screamed at Father, while Mother looked on fearfully and with exasperation. She could think of nothing to do. But Father could.

He shouted at me that I was a selfish, ungrateful child with no appreciation of all he sacrificed for us. "You will apologize immediately for your evil words," he shouted while balling his fists and mowing me down with his steely blue eyes. They could look as cold as a shoal of windswept Alaskan water in January. I hissed back at him that he could wait till hell froze over before I'd apologize for letting him know how much I missed everything that he and Mother had taken from me.

"That does it. You are out the door right now," he bellowed.

That might have been just fine with me except that I happened to have been in my underpants and a tattered old t-shirt. No matter. He grasped my arm and escorted me out the front door with considerable force, left me in the hall and returned, locking the door.

There can be nothing more ferocious than rage that cannot be vented. I stood in the hall, trembling with white-hot anger, humiliation, fear of discovery and vicious thoughts of revenge. I would take a knife and carve out his innards while he slept. I would relish eviscerating his heart and tossing it to wild dogs in the wilderness. I would plunge a dagger deep into his throat and watch the blood shoot angry and hot into a sky that was hungry for fireworks.

But my rage was to be a silent one. I could not risk a single sound for fear one of the other apartment doors would open to a half-naked girl cowering by a door that surely had no welcome mat. My stifled sobs brought Mother to the door and I saw it open to a shaft of light from the river that reflected the last evening light.

As Manfred began college at New York University, I was enrolled in a fine private school for girls on the banks of the Hudson River.

Gaining admission was no small feat as I was subjected to hours of testing at an off-campus center. I did so poorly on the intelligence test that the school's principal wondered openly how I had managed to make a bright, alert impression during the initial interview. Luckily I was called in for a second interview to discuss, among other things, why I did not know that cousins are the children of one's aunts and uncles and that a grandmother is the mother of one of one's parents.

Somehow, with no exposure to any relatives throughout my early life, my parents had neglected to enlighten me about relations. It was clear to me in a flash of hot shame, that I was ignorant of some very basic knowledge, which thrust me back into a kind of marginal social status in my mind: a developmentally retarded foreigner with much catching up to do. I was also keenly aware of having come from a southern public school where people were considered to "speak funny". I knew, of course, that "funny" didn't mean humorous. Funny was out of step, foreign and Appalachian without mountain majesty.

The accent, my original ticket to acceptance in the South, now definitely had to go. Mother's words about being flexible reverberated in my head and began to ring just a bit truer but certainly not because *she* had spoken them.

Miss Cooper, the tall, stern principal with dark, keen eyes, directed them like searchlights from me to Mother as we sat humbly in her office during that second interview. "She is a bright child, I think, as a matter of fact, possibly *quite* bright." She spoke as though I was not present in the room and that was fine with me. I flushed with quiet satisfaction and a small measure of pride while wishing to disappear entirely and never set foot on that green and gray campus again. It was a mixed bag in my view: lovely vitas and old trees like back on the farm but altogether too much somber, joyless appraising of my person. I was also sure that none of the kids had ever seen a horse. How wrong I was!

I felt vulnerable, like a misfit and a curiosity as Miss Cooper asked when we had come to America and why we had landed in Cuba, then below the Mason Dixon Line. In retrospect, I think she was genuinely interested, perhaps even mildly fascinated by the bits of our odyssey that she was able to tease out of Mother.

We certainly didn't fit the post-war bill of immigrants, especially not as former German government officials. One must credit Miss Cooper with having had a widely open mind and generous spirit or perhaps she simply overlooked the less than heroic stance my father had taken by remaining employed till nearly the end of the war.

If I close my eyes, I can remember that immigrant-child whose identity was still colored garishly by her family, separate while in the midst of a new, longed-for world. Father's poor English and his hopeless incomprehension of American thought and American ways had marked me deeply.

He could not embrace his new country; he could only draw parallels to his own and conclude that he was on very foreign soil. Mother retreated into anxious humility, never shedding a sense of being merely in transit—a fortunate guest at a table that had welcomed her charitably as a refugee of a monstrous war. The host, she felt, could not possibly make her an authentic member of a regular guest list. That is what it meant to her to be German after Hitler.

I started school in Riverdale with my neck tucked deeply into my collar as though a guillotine loomed above the crown of my head. Initially, I was politely skirted by my classmates as though I were a rare specimen from the Amazon: strange enough to keep at a distance but a curiosity on a dull day.

I was grateful for every moment that no one noticed me. I didn't mind lunching alone in the sunny dining room with its many windows looking onto a grassy slope. Greenery made me dream of Louisville and I inhaled our pasture and the scent of fresh hay as though it were within the reach of my extended hand.

I gravitated towards those girls who did not wear clothes from Saks Fifth Avenue and there was a comforting number who did not. I liked the shy girls who didn't win popularity contests or speak up in class before they were addressed.

I remember a sweet girl named Dolores who had stunning long hair the color of polished mahogany. It shone on the dullest of days and flipped up in a lovely soft layer of waves. She was Italian and her father was a hairdresser who took no small interest in her appearance. Dolores looked very stylish in homemade clothes that made my limited wardrobe look woefully out of step with the bobby-socked, hoop-skirted 1950s.

Mother dressed me in what she fancied, which insured that I looked like thirty going on twelve. A virginal white blouse and a homemade tweed skirt was no match for a classmate's trendy sweater that featured a clothesline across its front with items sporting the words, "My heart pants 4 U". Now *that* was cool and an attention grabber *par excellence*, not that I wanted attention just yet. But I did want to be cool.

I recall that camel hair coats were very much in fashion during my second year at the pretty school by the river. They were soft and smooth to the touch, casually chic and usually adorned with a long, colorful wool scarf. Everyone seemed to have one except me, which made me feel like a stand-in at a freak show—certainly not regular. I longed to look like my classmates, blending into the sea of camel-beige that wandered between buildings for classes on chill afternoons. While in the classroom, I felt reasonably a part of the scene because the focus was on our schoolwork, which proved to be no problem for me.

But during recess and between classes, the chatter was often about clothes and "cute boys," two topics on which I had little to contribute that I was willing to talk about. I had buried Morrie deep and safe where no light could penetrate and reveal that he had ever existed in my life. Tommy had become a distant memory though his horse trotted alongside Red in my cherished recollections of the fields at the farm. I was sure no one wanted to hear about them and surer yet that I would be seen as a hapless hayseed if I even mentioned Louisville. Besides, my memories were too precious to risk possible defilement.

Instead, those camel hair coats became a near-obsession, a ticket to inclusion in the only club I longed to join. I pleaded with Mother to buy me one but upon investigating their cost, she explained that she simply could not afford to buy me one.

She had a better plan, or so she thought. After rummaging through a collection of fabrics she had transported half way around the world, she found yards of horrifyingly genuine camelhair cloth she had bought at an open-air market in Turkey in the early 30s. When she showed me the bolts of cloth and shared her plans to make me a coat, my heart sank like a stone at sea.

It is no exaggeration to say that the fabric was not only coarse but also shockingly *hairy*. It looked as though an aging prehistoric beast had been stripped of its winter coat with not so much as a perfunctory grooming beforehand. I stammered something half vague and heartsick, indicating that the cloth looked nothing like the smooth and silken finish of the coats at school. Instantly I felt ashamed of myself, ungrateful and hurt, both for Mother and for me. In fact, I was nearly overwhelmed with a rush of competing, conflicting emotions, none of which felt good.

The coat's creation had been set into motion not unlike the inexorable development of a caterpillar that failed somehow to become a butterfly. Aside from its coarse, shaggy yak nap, if you can call it that, the coat was lovingly fashioned with a round collar more suited to a blouse, had no gracefully drooping half-belt in the back and sported large horn buttons one might find on a Bavarian hunting jacket. I looked about as strange among the young "sophisticates" of my class as a Chinese farmer at a Paris fashion show.

I wore it to school the first time on a chill late October day, feeling as though I blended into the carpet of dry brown leaves that blew across the lawns and gathered against the fences by the river. I felt like a furry forest animal of indeterminate species and I hurried into the building to wedge my coat inconspicuously between the satiny beige coats and colorful scarves, draping a classmate's maroon and white scarf across one of the hairy arms of my coat.

I must credit my classmates with admirable tact and sensitivity for not one derogatory word was said about my coat. It was ogled with some interest and one girl called it "unusual" in a way that indicated more genuine curiosity than derision.

In one way, the care taken not to hurt me was almost as painful as mockery might have been. I felt their pity and shame scalded me in sharp flashes. My agony remained a secret from all, particularly Mother. I wonder if she ever suspected that the coat had become a mantle of shame, an acknowledgement of strangeness. Turkish markets could be no match for Saks Fifth Avenue right then.

Teenage Turmoil

Despite my oddities, I was beginning to make friends. I began to like the feisty girls who always seemed to find something against which to rally. The issues were no weightier than a teacher's request that we follow a certain rule without questioning it.

The Librarian once had the "audacity" to say, "That's just the way it is. During study hour, there is no talking." Of course that became a direct invitation to chatter incessantly in strident voices. When reprimanded, we would imitate her aging, quavering voice and congratulate one another on having put her on the defensive. If only I could ask her forgiveness today as I recall her sweet and often perturbed expression at our cruelties. Undoubtedly she was wise enough to know that we were testing our limits, our independence, our ability to challenge authority.

I had more need than most to challenge authority since there was such a hefty portion of it at home. Growing up German in my family in the 1950s was an entry ticket to a Gulag, in my experience. Father left no room for even the most modest personal freedoms such as the ability to express one's opinions and, God forbid, to disagree with parental decrees. Children were, in actual fact, there to be only seen and not heard. I hope you will forgive my citing such a tired, worn out cliché. But then, it was a reality soon to become a terrible metaphor for repression of an even wider sort.

Social events that my classmates engaged in were off limits for me. Why, I challenged? "Because that is the way we do it in this family. You are too young to mix with those ill-mannered, common American boys from whom you will only learn bad habits," Father declared in a raised, agitated voice. Little did he know that ill manners had included physical violations at the hand of a middle-aged pedophile. I shudder to think what he would have done to me as well as Morrie had he known our dark secret. I feel certain he would have believed that I had brought on the advances on my breasts and pubic area and that he would have plunged me into even deeper shame and guilt than I already carried.

My evenings and weekends in those early months were lonely and given to reading anything I could get my hands on. Charles Dickens made me feel particularly good because many of his characters were in even direr circumstances than I was. I was comforted by the knowledge that I was not alone, for their lives were as real to me as those of my schoolmates.

There was also Marilyn Monroe to study, a waif turned adulated bombshell, the fantasy object of every male in my world and definitely someone to be emulated by the time I turned fourteen. I still have an old photograph that Manfred took of me with his Brownie camera. In it I am seated on our tiny front lawn in the house we later rented, posing as Marilyn would, head thrown back, chest thrust forward. I am wearing unrevealing jeans and a T-shirt but a come-on look that would have titillated only a teenage boy in hormonal overdrive. I cannot recall whether I picked the pose or whether he scripted it with his directions. He must have been twenty, too old to toy with or indulge the budding sexuality of his little sister.

In the midst of my Marilyn phase, I met Henry, known to most as Hank. He was a slender blond boy, one year older than I with intense, nervously scanning indigo eyes. He turned them my way one summer afternoon—a Saturday, I believe, and kept them on me for the next three years.

I was flattered by his attentions though more partial to the swarthy, dark Italian fellows who roamed our new neighborhood, which was a modest one on the north end of the leafy grand streets with their sprawling, turreted Tudor homes and generous Spanish-style villas.

Our street had a quaint charm with its small houses and hilly incline at the bottom of which was the tiny brick home we rented. Small new-growth trees cast modest shadows on the rutted, neglected sidewalks that undulated from the roots that lifted them and transformed some stretches into cemented mini hills.

Occasionally an elderly man set up his easel near our house and struggled to capture the quiet, unassuming small town feel of our little corner of Riverdale. The street, grandly named Sylvan Avenue, would have been more aptly called Sylvan Lane. Hyperbole did not become our neighborhood and was certainly not required. The street held its own as a painterly island in the center of considerable old-world wealth marked by wide tree-lined streets and sweeping, emerald lawns. In contrast, our tiny square of lawn was shaded by several untended, unruly pines and graced with two sprawling red azalea bushes that presided over a sea of deep green hues, mostly marauding ferns.

Henry did not live in our immediate vicinity but was drawn, as many local kids, into our neighborhood by a companionable corner drugstore with a small soda fountain. It served chocolate and vanilla egg creams, a New York institution of the 1950s and earlier that I recall as a watery, sweet, carbonated concoction sucked noisily and slowly through a straw while stealing furtive glances at one's neighbor on the next stool. The shop was unimaginably called Junior's Corner, situated on a strategic intersection and run by someone everyone knew as Junior.

Many a tryst was arranged at Junior's, many a tall tale told and even one teenage marriage began its rocky course there. They were both sixteen when Gina got pregnant and Quentin did the honorable thing.

The news rocked and rattled our little group of Irish and Italian teens as we danced to Bill Haley's rousing beat and knew that abstinence was still the only safe way to remain care free. We gathered at a Community House that had a swimming pool and canned music to dance to on summer nights under harsh lights and a soft moon.

Henry was there often with his buddies, including a few neighborhood hoods with names like Pancho, Frankie and Ron the Don. But I could only manage to slip out rarely past eight-thirty in the evening, my curfew. When I did, it was accomplished by walking to the end of our short street and, through carefully laid plans earlier in the day, jump into the waiting car of one of the older boys who saw himself as a brave liberator for Father was reviled as the Gulag warden that he'd become.

It soon became clear to me that he saw his own unbridled sexuality as inexorably imprinted on me, imagining me as the wild child in danger of wasting herself on the preying "delinquents" whose seething, pulsing needs had them braying at our door. Naturally, I was of little more interest than any of the other girls parading around in very brief shorts and tight shirts opened to the bra line. But he didn't see it that way. Guarding and preserving my virginity became his obsessive mission and he subjected me to endless, indiscreet questions about my activities with "those uncultured, common American boys." His haughty, elitist attitude reminded us daily of our foreignness, our many marks of strangeness amidst the democracy of my new American life where few distinctions between family backgrounds were made.

In time, Father enlisted Manfred to gain my confidence and extract secrets of my activities. He was only too happy to oblige, finding the mission titillating though quite unrewarding as I had, in the meantime, a few secrets to guard closely. My breasts and genitals had announced themselves with welcomed outside help in ways that were certainly forbidden, which ensured that I was more silent than a stone on the subject.

And what of Father's preoccupations during that time? After the tumultuous and treacherous times in Turkey, Russia and China, his post in New York must have seemed tamer to him than an aging house cat. Looking back, I think he was bored and what better way to fill the hours, in his view, than to throw dinner parties for his colleagues and new contacts.

It seemed that every week, Mother was planning ambitious menus for the upcoming weekend on which anywhere from four to six people would be imported from Manhattan, courtesy of Manfred's "taxi service," which entailed trips into the city in his second-hand Ford to fetch the guests and then return them again sometime close to midnight when they were properly fueled with good German wines, (God forbid that any other nation be the supplier), and Russian vodka, both imported via the diplomatic route that offered good prices and reliable delivery.

Manfred and I were recruited to serve the guests at table and bring the brandy and cigars afterwards. I did not really mind doing so, nor did Manfred, as we were paid fifty cents an hour, a wage that we were given to understand as being the best our parents could do. We never questioned the pay and were happy to receive what we did.

The living room was soon enveloped in blue smoke while the voices of our guests grew louder and more animated, especially Father's. Mother engaged in charming, low-key conversations, mostly with the ladies, and elicited easy conversation from them through her solicitous and warm enquiries into their lives. She never asked too personal a question, starting always with a subject that was general but geared to the presumed interests of her conversationalist. I marveled at her instinctive graciousness that ensured an easy flow of talk that steered clear of even the slightest contentiousness.

Father, by contrast, relished topics that could engender a lively and often pugnacious exchange. Favorite topics were, of course, politics with catty, cutting remarks about colleagues or acquaintances following closely.

Mother's discomfort over these exchanges was painfully visible and she would literally slide to the edge of her seat as though she were preparing to leap up and intercede with soothing, conciliatory words. Nothing made her more uncomfortable than his ventures into animated discourses that were obviously controversial. Nothing amused and invigorated him more than those very discussions and a battle of ideas that he invariably thought he won. His victories, such as they were, generally were truces of politesse in deference to hosts that had obviously gone to great efforts to serve a fine meal and offer generous transport service for the 15-mile journey from and to Manhattan.

To witness Mother's easy grace in social situations at a time when I was awkward, shy and rebellious towards all conventional practices was discomforting for me and conflicted me mightily. On the one hand, I felt certain that I would never be able to maneuver as smoothly and seemingly without effort as she did in social situations, on the other, I felt disdain for what I saw as a wasteful social charade designed only to fill the weekend evening hours. But the truth is that had they not been filled in that manner, my Father would have spent those hours at his desk writing endless letters of longing to Freda. As it was, he was generating significant income for the United States Post Office with his numerous, bulging letters every week that required extra postage to carry their copious, torrid messages.

I speak with authority on the subject, for after Freda's death suitcases of lengthy letters from him were found by her oldest daughter, letters that dated back to our early years in New York as well as to the years in China. To the present day, they remain in my cousin's possession, unread by her in order to keep at bay her rage at my father and to push aside the sorrow she still feels today on behalf of her own father.

The year 1955 was to become a particularly tumultuous one for my parents' marriage. Father decided to travel to Germany in February and visit family and various old friends, none of whom he had seen in nearly two decades. He also scheduled a visit to Bonn to help chart his career path. Mother did not join him, which suited him just fine as he had also planned a trip to the Black Forest town of Freiburg to visit Freda and her family. I am certain that Mother sensed his plans, which he undoubtedly did not share in their particulars.

He was gone for six weeks, a time of great harmony and peace in our home. No dinner parties, no arguments, no volcanic outbursts in the evenings and on weekends. Mother caught up on her gardening, raking the flowerbeds in preparation for spring, washing curtains and taking time out to read several books. We had no television, another mark of our strangeness and I was the only one in my class who was unable to discuss the evenings' programs.

When he returned, Mother began her long retreat into diminished affection for our father and began instead a period of cool, dutiful attendance to his rudimentary needs. Nonetheless, I do recall several flare-ups at that time when she raised her voice to uncharacteristic decibels and told him that she wanted a divorce.

"As far as I am concerned, you are free to be with Freda. But you've got a job ahead to deal with her husband and the effect it will have on their children," she stated firmly and with a discernable note of *Schadenfroheit*, though carefully avoiding the word, "divorce" in this initial exchange.

But Mother did not get the desired reaction. "Nobody leaves me. I love two women equally and besides you will not receive a penny from me if we are no longer married," he bellowed, ever the bully.

Having always "been the law" at home, he had no regard for outside laws that might be imposed on his family. Instead, he followed faithfully in the footsteps of his father who had, after all, thwarted all rules by simply living the life of an eccentric in a society that tolerated his willful quirkiness. It never occurred to Father that he might be held accountable, forced to pay alimony and child support, nor did it occur to Mother that the law would be able to support her against a tyrannical, philandering husband. The power of the fear he had so often engendered in her was crushing and paralyzing at this crucial time in their marriage.

They were both in the clutches of their own rules and myths, like orphaned children adrift in a dark Grimm fairy tale forest they couldn't see for the trees. Mother panicked and buckled under the threat of financial destitution, which seemed like a foregone reality to her.

Never having shaken the sense of being a foreigner who was merely a reluctantly tolerated guest in America, she could not accept that her status as a permanent resident, described at the time as a holder of an Alien Registration Card, entitled her to be protected by its civil laws just like everyone else. Hers was a feeling of profound vulnerability and national inferiority as a German citizen; Father's was one of unadulterated arrogance that recognized only the laws he made for himself and his family. Only years later did I realize that his mindset bordered on the psychotic, so vastly was he distanced from reality. In kinder moments I ponder whether reality was simply too harsh for an outwardly slumbering yet battered conscience.

I remember hoping that she would find the strength to leave him and never doubted that we would survive without his support. As weak as she was in the face of his onslaughts, I sensed her steely resolve to bring us through once he might be gone. She had cleaned houses before and would not hesitate to do so again if it came to that, I told myself with unwavering certainty.

Manfred was the witness who never took a stand. For one, he was largely preoccupied with himself and had also begun dating, a fact that we could only surmise from his occasional all-night absences. He did not volunteer any information on the way he spent his time nor was he asked. But Father seemed relieved to see his budding interest in girls, which had a tardy beginning at nineteen.

I thought it odd that he never uttered a word on the subject of our parents' strife nor voiced an opinion about Father's relationship to our aunt. But he did begin to show the first signs of double-standard thinking, condoning a man's infidelities as being a natural manifestation of maleness, in fact, a God given right. Our mother embodied for him the expected role of women to tolerate those sexual transgressions while remaining chaste and devoted to keeping a home together. He never questioned what he had witnessed for years and there was no sign that he ever thought about Mother's unmet needs. Besides, she seemed to carry on well despite her occasionally voiced dissatisfactions with Father.

Right before Father's departure for Germany, I said to Manfred that I found Father selfish in pursuing his pleasures while Mother was expected to carry on for weeks without adequate funds; Father had declared that he needed February's salary for the trip and she would have to manage on less money till he returned.

"He needs a break," was the ill-considered curt answer Manfred gave, adding, "I think he also very much needs to see Aunt Freda." Hard to dispute that, of course, if you considered just Father's requirements, I muttered under my breath. I remember lapsing into unsettled silence at the realization that my brother and I stood on distant shores from one another on a fundamental issue of growing concern to me.

I was everything other than "sweet sixteen" during that tense year whose early spring had offered the sweet contrast to our daily life afforded by Father's lengthy absence. I had tasted what life could be like without him and it was good. I began to openly despise him for his selfish, despotic rule over us. To make matters worse, he had increased his surveillance of my life outside our home.

My curfew was eight-thirty, generally giving me just an hour after supper to slip out and join the regular crowd at Junior's. There we would perch like birds on a wire upon the stools at the soda fountain, our eager faces made unnaturally bright by the neon light of a Coca Cola sign behind Junior. He seemed always to be wiping the shiny Formica surface of the bar with an oversized towel and straining to hear our excited, hushed re-telling of the day's stories.

Henry would casually drape a possessive arm over my shoulders whenever one of the other boys would sidle over and start a conversation with me as though to say, "I will tolerate your presence as long as you know that I have claimed her." I resented his public claim on me as it interfered with my flirtations and helped create a painfully accurate picture of my flighty nature.

It was a time of unfurling for me, of discovery of my power, such as it was, and a way to scorn the rules of my parents. I secretly wished to be a "wanton slut", desired by many while I selectively withheld my favors. I dreamed of unbridled passion and a come-on look like Marilyn Monroe's while granting only a grazing of my nipples by a boy's lips. I had no courage for more.

In the solitary hours after my curfew, I sat in my small mansard room and poured into a diary all the dreams, frustrations, despair and floundering sexual exploits that filled my days. *My family are a bunch of misfits,* I wrote. *"Even Mother doesn't resemble other mothers in the slightest. She caves in to Father's medieval ways and finds fault with everything I do. The other day she poured my bottle of Shalimar perfume down the toilet, saying it had a cheap vanilla smell like whores would wear."*

I was particularly angry over that heavy-handed measure because I had received the perfume from my best friend at school for Christmas and in a rage I told her how much I hated her for trying to run every aspect of my life. Then I hurled her favorite Elizabeth Arden face cream out the window onto the stone terrace below where it splattered most satisfactorily and visibly. I dealt the final blow by saying she was no better than Father.

My diary's most salacious passages were recorded in a reversed-letter code not unlike Pig Latin. They recounted bumbling sexual explorations with Henry, which I saw as very daring and advanced. A hand on my breast, brave fingers trailing my inner thigh, his tongue in my ear, were more exciting and forbidden than anything either of us could imagine at that time.

I accommodated Henry's forays by wearing skirts rather than jeans, and panties that were silken to the touch. How depraved, I thought, but also how deliciously daring and rebellious! We were both certain that we were ahead of our time, advanced in our development, mature and ready for life. If someone would have openly called me a slut, I would have felt an icy thrill, a sense of triumph that I had lured, baited and enticed a boy as ready for ecstasy as I. One step closer to Marilyn, I dreamed.

No venue was too uncomfortable for our trysts, even in late fall after the first frost. In a rock-strewn stretch of woods with ice frosting the late patches of moss, we lay bruised and cold on the ground and satisfied our needs as best we could without risking pregnancy. To me, pregnancy was the maximum-security prison I vowed not to enter. It would transform my life into the shackled, conflicted existence of my parents. Of that I was certain.

And while much of this sexual agitation was being recorded in my diary and we continued our woodsy adventures, Henry and I were watched through binoculars by a teacher from my school whose apartment overlooked *our* woods, as we thought of them. Undoubtedly, it was the most exciting event in his solitary life and a vicarious pleasure he enjoyed for weeks before finally reporting our activities to the principal. I had finally fully earned a reputation of depravity and it would have dire consequences at the end of my junior year.

In the meantime I was to suffer Father's Grand Inquisition. Manfred had colluded with him in deciphering my carefully hidden diary and I was called upon to confess and elaborate on my sexual activities. Elaborate on them? Give details? Denial was the only path to take and I strode it with defiance.

"You have no right to invade my privacy and accuse me of things I have not done," I shouted at both of them. "What business is it of yours what I do in my free time? I have so little of it anyway, thanks to all your rules. None of my friends have parents who snoop through their drawers. We now live in America where our freedom is guaranteed."

Father shot back that American freedom for its children is what gave rise to such ill-mannered and undisciplined youth that had no respect for elders. "They roam the streets like untamed, wild animals and their parents impose no rules. Then, when they *are* home, they watch primitive television shows instead of reading and learning." For him, all of America was like Karl May's tales of the Wild West that Germans had devoured with an insatiable appetite. No matter that Karl May had never set foot in America when he wrote them.

There was yet another influence on his view of America. Upper class German families often sent family members to America if they did not conform to the expectations of their society or families: if they were renegades, free thinkers or not good scholars. So, America was not seen so much as a training ground as it was a place of exile where their offspring's "failures" would not embarrass their families. It was a place to sink or swim. A place of *material* opportunity where success could be cited as achievement back home but failure would never be a blemish as it could remain forever a secret. "If you don't behave (speak, toe the line) we'll send you to America," was not an uncommon threat in his world. Standards in America were seen as lower, no matter that values were simply different. You could always simply become a "Karl May cowboy" or, if a city dweller, you could wash dishes and work up to become Maitre D' or chef.

Father's preoccupation with my "sexual purity" culminated in a forced visit to a gynecologist, my first, to determine if I was still a virgin. I was enraged at the indignity of such an inquisition and wonder even today what the doctor thought of my parents and their priorities. With my virginity confirmed, Father's and Manfred's sleuthing diminished only slightly while my antagonism and rebelliousness rose to new levels of heat. I didn't waste a single opportunity to show my disdain for all three of my captors, for I saw myself as a prisoner whose sentence would be up at the first chance I could seize to leave home.

Also vivid among my recollections was a dreadful Sunday in the country when Manfred was charged with chauffeuring the family up to a nearby park in the Bear Mountains for "fresh air and recreation". Nothing could have been further from what I might have planned for the afternoon. I had no qualms about the destination; it was decidedly the company I resented, particularly that of my father.

No sooner did we ascend to a modest peak overlooking rolling hills dotted with pines and a sunny meadow that ended in a vast parking lot, but Father decided to launch a bellowing lecture on my selfishness, depravity and the worries I caused the family. I dubbed it "The Sermon on the Mount" with an ironic nod to its self-serving worldliness. The designation stuck, for all time. Its one gift was the laughter it engendered even decades later and I must give Father credit for his appreciation of the irony I had pinpointed. On occasion he was able to be mildly self-deprecating.

That evening, I developed a very high temperature and aches throughout my entire body. I lay in a fever for days until I was finally diagnosed with polio. In those first days I experienced a frightening episode of seeing myself outside my body, looking down from a corner in the ceiling onto my still form on the sheets. I fought hard to reunite with my body and finally felt my fear subside as I became whole again. It is no surprise that the illness struck at a time when I was filled with paralyzing rage and despair. A low point of crippling magnitude had finally been achieved.

There is no need to linger unduly on the months that followed—months of physical therapy and a fierce will to regain control of my left leg, which bore the final brunt of the disease. I owe an immense debt of gratitude to a woman filled with the strength and light of healing who came daily to work with me as I fought to regain strength. Naehma was the daughter of a renowned Austrian writer, Richard Beer-Hofmann and a personal friend of Martin Buber. But above all, she was a deeply loving person whose life force spread its mantle of strength and healing over everyone whose lives she touched and there were many.

Her exercises were playful and highly imaginative in their child-like images. I was called upon to be a rabbit, ready to spring, a bird preparing for flight, a cat poised to pounce. And I soared with her even as tears of frustration at my helplessness washed my face. At those times she would cradle my head in her large, soft arms and say, "*Kindl*, you will be swift as a rabbit escaping a fox in no time. And you will soon be able to mount a horse again."

She had a sure instinct for what truly motivated me and I dreamed on many nights that I was able to lift my strengthening left leg to the height of Red's stirrup and swing up effortlessly. In those nights I flew with him across endless sunny fields, my arms around his neck, my cheek in his mane.

While that day never returned to my waking hours, I did get strong enough to ride many other horses in later years, even abroad. One particularly memorable morning in the *Pfalz* region of Germany, I rose at six to ride through the vineyards of the *Buerklin* wine estate and watch a young deer bound into the undergrowth as I galloped by. I was awash in joy, flooded with happiness. Thank you, dearest Naehma, poet's daughter and healer, for the bliss you made possible.

And then it was 1956 and it was good to be healthy and strong again. Polio was a pale memory, there was always enough food on our table and, for the first time, I felt that there was continuity to our lives: that we would stay and build on what we had.

School friends were there again each September no matter where they had been all summer. I loved the stories of their European adventures, a month in France to improve grammar and pronunciation, two months of music camp in New England for the gifted singer or a summer of sports on a New Hampshire lake.

I cannot deny that I was also envious but by the same token, I never expected that summers of adventure could be mine. In my consciousness, I stood firmly outside such opportunities and that feeling was so deeply ingrained as to have become a part of the very image I had of my person. Such summers were for Americans with deep roots in a land of plenty and opportunity, a land I was certain was not accessible to a fledgling American. I cannot remember if I believed then that I would *ever* graduate from my vividly held immigrant status. And no one told me I would.

My teenage years were drawing toward a close, hastened by an event that took me once again into a new, unwished for environment. From his lofty window overlooking our woods, the lone man with binoculars continued his watch and finally reported me to the principal for "lewd activities". I reasoned later that envy finally got the better of him and the only cure was revenge.

My parents were summoned by Miss Cooper and told that my behavior was inappropriate for a young lady attending such a fine school and was the final straw in a series of rebellious and incendiary activities towards several of the teachers. "We have been very patient with Vera," she added, "but our school is no longer the right place for her. We urge you to seek out another place from which she can graduate next year."

Clearly, my school did not want an alumnus like me on their rolls and, while I could not blame them, I was also enraged and heartbroken. I was about to lose a small but close group of buddies whose friendship I valued deeply and who had contributed significantly to the scaffolding of my shaky self-esteem. They also had helped me solidify a value system for which I had the courage to fight. In that system, one did not accept without question the standards and principles others imposed. No book would ever be evaluated by its flyleaf: no persons by their origin, religion or skin tone. And Father would never be the arbiter of laws governing my life, of that I was certain.

Oak Grove, an obscure Quaker girls' school in Maine outside of Waterville accepted me, primarily for my good singing voice as there was no one in that year's senior class who could sing the soprano solo in Gounod's *Sanctus*, a long-held graduation tradition there. It also helped that my grades were good and were able to offset the reputation that I was bringing with me as described in my transfer papers. The word "spirited" was *not* used as a substitute for "incendiary" and "rebellious".

I was to spend a painful year marked by despair and bitterness in the drafty halls of that boarding school amongst girls from broken marriages, many homesick and unhappy. To make matters worse, the headmistress was an elderly, despotic disciplinarian who had not yet entered the twentieth century and imposed a multitude of draconian rules.

We wore blue uniforms and cumbersome oxford shoes, were exposed to endless sermons about morality in frequent visits to a small chapel on the grounds, were told that smoking ranked right up with the sins of the flesh and were spied upon by members of the school government council, which was charged with reporting any transgressions to the headmistress.

During the first three months, I was as lonely as a wolf separated from her pack. The school was a vast, daunting brick structure on a windy hill overlooking a meadow ringed by dense forest. There were barns for the horses of girls who were deserving of riding privileges but my rebellious attitude soon insured that I was not one of them. In my state of not so quiet rage, I did the only thing I knew: thwart all the rules and thumb my nose at anyone with authority.

Since smoking was strictly forbidden, I introduced candy cigarettes to room parties and was seen smoking an actual cigarette on the train from New York to Maine. Immediately, I was sentenced to a kind of quarantine that forbade me any visits to Waterville, a weekly privilege for the obedient, as well as entry into the stables where I longed most to be. Mrs. Owens, our headmistress, had an uncanny way of knowing what was most meaningful to each student. Withholding pleasures was her specialty.

As an exercise in gaining social graces, there were two annual dances with Hebron Academy, a repository of nerdy, pimply boys in our view. You had to be very lonely or bored to look forward to those events.

Before each dance, each girl's gown was inspected by Mrs. Owen and its distance from the ground measured with a large, officious ruler. Too long was dramatic and unseemly; too short was wantonly alluring.

I was not subjected to this inspection as dances were ruled out for me as part of my punishment for having been seen with a cigarette. But that did not keep me from openly ridiculing the dress inspections. I was quickly joined by others whom I was considered to have incited. My reputation seemed to grow worse by the week and it garnered me the friendship of the more daring, angry and outspoken girls. If I was going to be miserable there, I might as well let everyone know it by opposing the rules, I reasoned.

At Thanksgiving, I was not invited home by my family, a stunning blow, so Christmas became the next longed for time to see my New York friends. My roommate, the pretty daughter of an apple farmer near Augusta, generously extended an invitation for me to come home with her for the holiday and I accepted gratefully. The weekend proved to be wonderfully regenerative. I met a neighbor who was a poetry writing, thoughtful student, home from Exeter Academy for Thanksgiving. His letters during the last six months of my austere existence at Oak Grove were a lifeline to a saner more contemplative life; he wrote well and often.

The next milestone was marked during the Christmas holiday at home, just days after I returned to a less than enthusiastic welcome. I was seen as a returning problem, which is also how I saw my parents but had ceased to care, being far more focused on seeing Henry and other friends.

Henry was also home for the holidays from his first year at *William and Mary College*. But he was very ill with mononucleosis and our contact was restricted to ardent phone conversations in which we reaffirmed our love for one another as only teenagers in hormonal tumult can.

A week before Christmas, I attended a holiday dance at our local church without him, looking forward to seeing many other friends, one of whom was a respectful admirer who had waited patiently in the sidelines for me to tire of Henry. Ron was handsome and gentle and I had more than a passing interest in him, in part because my parents found him utterly unacceptable: he was from a working class Italian family and had a younger brother who was notorious for his run-ins with the law. No matter that Ron was sweet, responsible and planning to go to college.

The evening in the church's activity room was to turn into a night of horror. I was decidedly on a trajectory of misfortune without the longer, more thoughtful perspective on such a path that adulthood can offer.

During a pause in the music and after a slow dance with Ron during which we seemed to simply lean into one another, I excused myself to call Henry from the adjoining Parish House. My intent was to cheer him up and, undoubtedly, to allay my guilt over a growing attraction to Ron.

I turned on the light, dialed Henry's number and asked his mother if I could speak to him. After less than a minute, he came to the phone. Just then the light extinguished and left me in near darkness except for a garden lantern's faint light through the trees. Like a feral animal in the wild, I knew in an instant that I was in grave danger.

There is an unforgettable way in which fear shows its face in the heart of near darkness. You can smell it, you can feel and it leaves you with a shuddering chill at the base of the spine. And so it was for me on that December night, even before I heard a deep, male voice say, "I'd like to use the phone after you."

I stammered a weak, "yes" and Henry asked who was with me. Before I could answer, a tall figure lunged towards me across the shadowy space. I must have dropped the phone to raise my arms above my head just seconds before a loud crack reverberated through me and the room tilted upwards to meet me: Flashes of light, then darkness.

I awoke to gaze into the kind black face of an ambulance attendant dressed in white. "You'll be fine, Miss. We're going to the hospital now," he said in a steady reassuring voice. And then his face merged with that of my assailant and I felt another bolt of fear surge through me. Mercifully, I blacked out again on the stretcher.

When I awoke, I was being rolled into the hospital, vaguely aware of a pain in my left wrist where five gold bangle bracelets had been crushed into my skin by the blows from a hard object. My head was numb, as though nothing existed on top of my neck. It was a sweet mercy—until the emergency room doctor began to sew my fractured skull, which had regained feeling by then. I am not given to screaming but on that night, sounds tore from my throat that had an inhuman, wild sound. Between breaths and throughout, I prayed to die.

I spent that night in a nauseous haze of morphine and was visited by both a priest and a rabbi who each prayed with me and held my hands gently in theirs.

Later I learned that Ron, hearing my screams, had rushed into the room and wrestled my assailant to the ground. He tied the man's hands with his belt. The doctors later told my parents that there could be little doubt that Ron had saved my life that night. Over the years I have sent him my thanks in silent prayers for I have lost track of his whereabouts.

At home again, I was installed much of the day on the living room sofa, making mealtimes easier for Mother with no stairs to climb. I had to remain nearly motionless for ten days because of the severe concussion I had suffered. Voices around me were hushed, favorite dishes prepared and much ice cream served. But I longed to be up and out of the house with my friends.

My recovery was remarkably swift and with the exception of unexpected bouts of acute anxiety whenever someone walked closely behind me, I moved beyond the event by focusing on the good fortune of having had such a protective friend in Ron. Father reluctantly admitted to that good fortune and designated Ron as my *Lebensretter* or lifesaver, thanking him with genuine feeling for his courage and swift action.

And yet it was not too soon for Father to voice a wish that would "make him very proud and happy". On my first day up, he announced that he had been asked if I could represent Germany at the upcoming International Debutante's Ball to be held at the old Astor Hotel and in the spring, join the group of girls and their chaperones on a whirlwind tour of Paris and London. There were dances and parties scheduled in both cities as well as sightseeing and a visit to the Ascot Races.

Nothing could have been more contrary to my rebel's sensibilities. I was aghast at the elitist, superficial, class-oriented spirit of the events and deeply embarrassed at the prospect of being seen in such a setting, for I knew some newspapers would cover the festivities in New York.

I was to share the bill with a French Countess, an American heiress and an English daughter of the knighted class, to name just a few of the "luminaries". Of course, I was to be announced and listed as Baroness von Saucken, which caused me the deepest embarrassment, especially since the title was an exaggeration. We were missing the requisite number of spikes in the crown of our coat of arms to justify the title of Baroness, but no matter, as far as the committee for the events was concerned. It was, after all, about luster, the kind that needn't have much staying power.

The night Father announced that I *would* attend the event as Miss Germany (and there was no room for doubt or discussion in his mind), we were seated at the dinner table, he to my right and Mother across from me. Manfred sat to my left in a familiar slouch and wearing a non-committal expression on his face, lest he be asked to take sides in what was destined to become a violent dispute.

I stated emphatically that I would be no part of such a phony, hollow, un-American folly, rife with monarchy overtones. Father laid down his knife and fork and fixed me with his steely violet eyes. There was a resounding silence, the kind that stills the land before a tornado strikes. And then he said: "You *will* attend and makes us all proud. This is a wonderful opportunity that you are too young to grasp."

I shot back that I was not too young to distinguish between worthwhile appearances that endorsed the right principles and ones that were foolish, superficial rituals that belonged in a former century and not in America, the land of equality. My idealism was, of course, born of youth, zeal and fresh discovery.

That is when his fists balled into two firm, pugnacious heaps on either side of his place setting and the corners of his mouth turned down like a sinister half moon on its ear. I do not recall exactly how the glass of water I held left my hand so rapidly and headed for his face, dead on. He ducked just in time and it shattered the glass of an eighteenth century Chinese print, which hung just behind him.

He rose slowly, deliberately and menacingly from his chair and, taking a deep breath to add suspense, declared in a voice as chilling as a death rattle, that I was to leave *his* house immediately.

"I don't care if you end up in the gutter as a whore or what you do with your life. I will give you five hundred dollars to start you on whatever way you chose to take…and that is all you will receive. I am finished with you."

I felt a swift rush of hope followed by a surge of anxiety and then relief at the prospect of freedom from Father's oppressive, iron hand. I would make it on my own, I vowed.

But it was not to be. Mother shot out of her chair and declared in a trembling voice that if I were to be expelled, she would leave with me never to return. There was a dead silence as I stormed from the room and prepared to pack a few belongings. I never heard the heated words between them that followed but I could hear my father's bellowing voice overshadowing Mother's plaintive arguments on my behalf. I no longer cared about either of them. I wanted simply to be free, wild as winter winds across open fields and I abandoned myself to dreams of struggles won in a world that welcomed me and friends that would reach out to help me find my way. All the while, I packed.

Less than an hour passed before Mother ran up the stairs and announced that she had negotiated a peace. Father had said that I could stay if I apologized for my behavior. Darkness descended on me as though the sun had been extinguished by a great natural catastrophe and I sat down on the edge of my bed and wept uncontrollably.

Then I said, "I will never apologize for expressing my opinions to which I have as much right as he does to his. We live in a free country whether he knows it or not. I have rights and I will exercise them."

"Your father awaits an apology and our family will fall apart if you do not say the right words," she said in a sad and grave voice. Clearly, she was afraid to leave with me, though she would have done so if I refused to help her build at least a makeshift bridge to peace. I was between two sizable boulders and, in her uncertainty and anxiety, Mother was not able to spare me a bitter decision. I told her that I needed time to think in solitude. I wanted her gone and she knew it so she slipped out the door on silent soles.

I don't know how long I sat paralyzed on my bed, thoughts racing through my mind like frantic birds caught in a net. And then I decided what to say.

I knew I would find Father in the living room, blowing blue cigarette smoke into a white space. I descended the stairs slowly and paused in the doorway.

"I am sorry for the angry way in which I expressed my feelings," I uttered in a flat but clear voice, knowing that he would choose just to hear the words, "I am sorry". They would liberate him from his threat and ensure that Mother would stay with him. I was palpably a secondary issue in the matter but that did not matter much to me in that moment. What mattered was the despair that washed over me as I realized that I would not yet be able to leave home. Too much rested on my departure. And then a hard knot of anger formed in the pit of my stomach. It was to lodge there, unforgiving like a stone, for years to come.

Father had asked me to sit down across from him. He paused with portend then slowly and deliberately extinguished his cigarette.

"I accept your apology," he said curtly, adding that my behavior had been unacceptable. "That shall never happen again in my house," he finished. We stared at each other in silence and I rose to leave the room and call Henry. He was not home.

Inevitably, the matter of the Debutante Ball resurfaced and Mother asked our doctor if I would be well enough to attend. It was decided that I had made remarkable progress and would be fit for all the Christmas holiday events.

By that time, I had ceased caring whether I attended or not; as a matter of fact, part of me welcomed the chance to be out from under parental supervision for I knew they would not be attending the parties, only the Ball. I could live with that since they would be seated far from where all the young people would be.

Mother arranged for me to model a gown for Saks Fifth Avenue with a credit for the store listed in the program. We were, of course, not able to afford a gown.

I chose an off-the-shoulder gown of white Damask silk. The matching heels pinched my feet but gave me a feeling of stature and grace though it was a struggle not to topple from their two-inch height. There was also the danger of catching a heel in the hem of the floor length gown so my mind was preoccupied on the night of the Ball with avoiding embarrassments. A trickle of perspiration made its way down the back of my neck as my name was called and I stepped hesitantly onto the dance floor withy Ken, my handsome, dark flag-bearer from Annapolis Naval Academy. Blinded by the popping flashbulbs, the announcer's words echoing in my ear, "Miss Germany, Baroness Vera von Saucken," I fought to show confidence and grace amidst the self-assured lovely girls who shared the spotlight with me. I was possibly the only girl that night who had never been to a glamorous party or Ball and I was keenly aware of my inexperience but determined to hide it.

It did not help my confidence that my hair was precariously arranged to hide the wound and shaved area, which formed a small half-circle across the middle of my head.

I was particularly intimidated by the slender, pretty girl who represented France. She was self-assured and charming, flirtatious and genteel in the way she moved amongst the escorts that bore the flags of their schools. I watched and took mental notes, staying close to Ken who was protective and reassuring; I had mentioned my accident to him for fear that he would wonder about my odd hairdo. His response was a gentle squeeze of my shoulders as he told me how lovely I looked.

As the evening wore on, my gratitude and admiration for his easy grace grew notably. I realized that I was in the company of a more sophisticated, subtle and finely tuned young man than I had ever known and I vowed to rethink my goals and dreams after the festivities were over. It was a strong wish that was to yield a small, delayed harvest. But where a seed is sown, new life will eventually push forth.

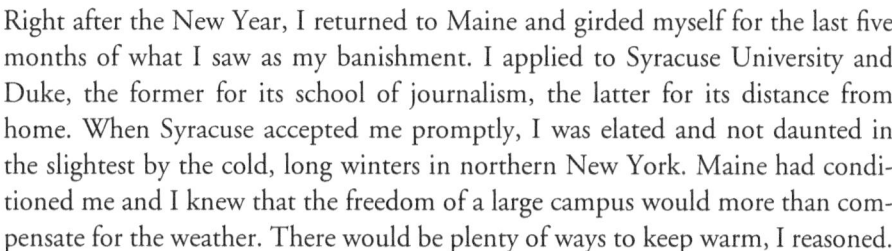

Right after the New Year, I returned to Maine and girded myself for the last five months of what I saw as my banishment. I applied to Syracuse University and Duke, the former for its school of journalism, the latter for its distance from home. When Syracuse accepted me promptly, I was elated and not daunted in the slightest by the cold, long winters in northern New York. Maine had conditioned me and I knew that the freedom of a large campus would more than compensate for the weather. There would be plenty of ways to keep warm, I reasoned.

What I did not count on was that my parents would have no part of my plan. In fact, they had quietly charted my next few years and those were to be out of the country. I will never know which of them had come up with the idea, though I suspect it was Father with Mother's ready consent for she felt powerless against my prevailing anger and wished me gone. Beyond that, she had embarked on a new project: helping Manfred through college as he was failing and quite disinterested in his studies.

Her efforts were heroic and she spent countess hours in libraries, doing his research, deciphering his class notes—even contacting his professors for guidance in how best to help him. When I learned of her efforts upon my return, I was stunned that such help was sanctioned by the professors and I can only conjecture that it was an unprecedented case for which no rules had been laid down by the university. Manfred did graduate, though it cannot have instilled much pride in him, especially not after Father sardonically congratulated *Mother* for her college degree.

Only weeks before my graduation, I received the news that I would not even be coming home for the summer and would not be attending Syracuse University in the fall. Rather, my parents would be bringing my most essential belongings with them in the car with Manfred as chauffeur and I would travel with Mother by boat from Canada to Germany for deposit with her family in Freiburg directly after graduation. I felt like a piece of baggage being moved about at the will of others. Destination: the home of my father's mistress.

I learned of my exile from a stern letter Father wrote. I took it outdoors and sat on the vast sweep of lawn that descended from the rambling brick structure that was our dormitory. With a sharp sense of foreboding, I reluctantly opened the envelope and read:

"Your mother and I have decided that you will benefit greatly from an extended stay in Germany with your mother's family in Freiburg. It is time that you absorb European culture, which has evolved over centuries in contrast to the very new, undeveloped, materialistic culture that we have here in America. You need to learn the lessons of discipline, a sense of history and respect for the long heritage that is our family's. The Sauckens can trace their roots back 800 years and we are related to Martin Luther..." and on it went with no mention of Mother's accomplished family. But I had stopped reading and crushed the pages in my fist. Father was not given to short expositions.

I was to live in Freiburg for two years and attend the *Gymnasium* or German high school to gain my *Abitur*, the equivalent of two years of college in America. That meant having to rapidly catch up in Mathematics, Latin and French, all subjects in which my German age group was more advanced than I despite my fine private schooling in New York. No one could have been less motivated for the task than a girl ready for college with plans to major in Journalism.

Surely Father was pleased with himself for having engineered a new link to his mistress. Now he could plan to visit me and give a face of respectability to encounters with Freda. Can Mother not have seen the ploy? Or did she simply no longer care? I just do not know and cannot ask her in these last months of her life. (As I write these words, she is ninety-six and frailer than anyone should have to be. I take comfort in the fact that she enjoyed the freedom of thirty-eight years of widowhood, a bittersweet gift, to be sure. But on balance, it worked out favorably for her.) Quite honestly, at the time I did not see through Father's Master Plan, being totally preoccupied with my readjustment to a new world and new challenges. His motives were of no interest to me, especially because I had become indifferent to Mother's plight. She was, after all, part of the conspiracy to send me away.

Graduation was a blur, a scene through a smudged lens. I was alternately numb, in pain and enraged at my powerlessness. I longed to be home with my friends, to at least say goodbye, to feel friendship and sympathy, to exchange promises to write and, yes, to feel good and sorry for myself.

Henry was stunned and outraged that we would not see each other for two years. He wrote me a poignant letter days before I left for Germany in which he declared that he would never forget me—that he would wait for my return no matter how long. We both wallowed in all the pathos and drama that was the mark of our generation's teen years. And, of course, we confused our longed for ecstasies in the dark for lasting love made more intense by separation. We might have been the last generation of teen dreamers who lived by the messages of their songs. We wrote our *Love Letters in the Sand* and silently mouthed the words of *My Prayer* for the one we loved.

When I stepped forward to sing the solo part in *Sanctus*, I trembled from the effort to control my voice, to keep it steady and on key. I did succeed modestly but as I stepped back to signal the entry of the chorus, I saw the faces of my family in the audience and was overcome by the sadness of my departure. My throat closed and I could only mouth the words. I would soon be three thousand miles away in a country praised by my parents for the discipline it imposed on young people. Often enough, they had recounted memories of their youth shortly after the turn of the twentieth century: the somber aunts, the foreboding uncles, the governesses with switches and rulers that stung their behinds when lessons were not learned or thank-you notes not written promptly. I fully expected to find draconian rules and severe punishments in my new home.

Discovering Germany

On a sunny early June day, Mother and I boarded an ocean liner on the St. Lawrence River destined for Bremen, Germany. No time was allotted to explore Montreal. That would have meant a night's stay in a hotel, an expense thought to be frivolous and unnecessary.

Manfred and Father waved from the pier, two dwindling figures in a mist of my tears of rage. I was glad to see them fade as we pushed away from land laboriously and headed towards the open sea. I stood on deck alone for a long time, feeling Father's tyranny fall away from me with every sea mile we conquered. But there was a tight knot of fear deep in my gut. Would I encounter as much severe discipline as Father meted out?

I pictured a nation of shouters who brandished rules and taboos like medieval knights wielding swords of steel. In my troubled thoughts, I was heading for the land that had sent millions to their deaths in gas chambers, had shot insurgents and conscientious objectors against Hitler's regime, whipped young children with belts and rulers, had censored the news media and inducted its young people into Hitler Youth Groups where they were taught to denounce those who did not back Hitler's ideals.

My relatives were still alive, a sign that I took to mean they had not objected to Hitler. Yes, the war had ended twelve years ago but did that mean that Germans were fundamentally different now? On the deck of that ship in 1957, I embraced every stereotypical judgment that had ever been leveled against post-war Germans. It suited my dark mood just fine to pass my own devastating judgment on the imagined prison I was about to enter. But real life was, of course, vastly different.

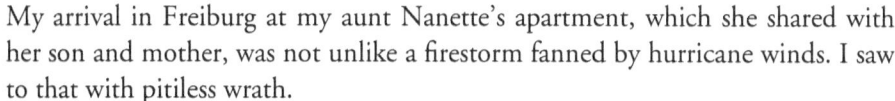

My arrival in Freiburg at my aunt Nanette's apartment, which she shared with her son and mother, was not unlike a firestorm fanned by hurricane winds. I saw to that with pitiless wrath.

Mother and I were seated across from each other and I glared at her with the meanest expressions I could muster. Then I announced to the room, "I do not wish to be here and I have not been asked by either of my parents how I feel about just being dumped here." I spoke in English to make it doubly difficult for my hapless relatives.

Then Freda arrived from her apartment above Nanette's. I held her gaze for longer than was comfortable for either of us. She eyed me suspiciously after our eye-lock and cast cautious glances at my mother. I disliked her instantly for her cool reserve in the presence of a sister she had betrayed for years. She did not even have the decency to show regret much less guilt, I thought: quite the contrary. She sat in an overstuffed chair, her back to the window that faced a grove of pine trees across the road and looked at my mother and me at regular intervals with a neutral, inscrutable expression.

Nanette then said in a calm, reasoned voice that she could understand how I felt but that I could also choose to see my stay as a new adventure with much to teach me. Mother chimed in that I was ungrateful for the opportunity to expand my horizon and quite unsuited for America in my present state of rebellion.

"She is out of control and we cannot handle her in her present frame of mind. She must learn a new perspective on life and far more self-discipline before she can become an adult," she added sternly.

Why, I wondered, did she think that this task should be transferred to relatives? It could only be that she wanted to be rid of me, did not care about my feelings and did not feel up to the task of being a parent.

I glared at Mother and told her that I hated her for not respecting my opinions and goals, for not allowing me to attend college in the States and for sending me back to a secondary school curriculum with kids who were a year younger than I. "You have demeaned me and forgotten that I am your daughter, not your pawn to move around on a chess board," I hissed at her.

By then I was oblivious to my aunts and when my grandmother entered the room, I looked up only briefly to acknowledge the tall, dignified figure that took her seat quietly and with remarkable composure in the midst of the icy détente we had reached. She had neat white hair piled on top of her head and wore a light gray dress that fell in soft folds to her ankles. I did not greet her, reveling in the fact that my insolence was unmistakable in its message.

"I have been taken away from all my friends and never once asked how that makes me feel," I continued. And then, just for good measure, I reached for a nearby vase and threw it across the room at Mother. It shattered at her feet where I had thankfully aimed in a chance moment of lucidity.

With that our meeting was adjourned and Nanette grimly accompanied my Mother and me upstairs to view the mansard room under the eaves where I was to live for the next several years. It was the only time I ever saw her warm dark eyes narrow in stern determination and a furrow etch deeply between her brows. We followed her agile steps up the old stone stairwell, her flowered skirt a bright swinging tapestry in the dusky afternoon light of dancing dust particles. She reached for the banister and I saw that her hand trembled slightly. In the ensuing years, I was to see only steady, confident hands.

How can Nannette and her mother not have resented the burden they were asked to carry? To this day I can only explain their acceptance of the yoke I was to be for the first months by the sense of familial duty they all carried with set jaws and strong shoulders. They had survived a war and they could certainly endure an enraged teenager, they must have told themselves.

Mother stayed only a few days and I made certain not to see much of her. I spent most of my time gazing out of my small window that looked westward over vine-yards to the *Voges* Mountains near the French border that was just a few kilometers away. I liked the idea of looking west and I soon came to love the gentle hills that were home to the Black Forest and the orchards that captured the afternoon light which lay like a soft gold spun blanket over the green of June in Germany that sum-mer.

But time often hung heavy in the voluntary isolation of that room. I would sit for hours at a heavy *Biedermeier* desk that had been installed for me and doodle on the ink blotter or pin art cards of Franz Marc's horses and deer on the walls in an attempt to recall the happy years on the farm. It was comforting to go backwards in time rather than to live in the moment. And during that first year in Freiburg, I longed once again for my China home and the sunny safety of my sixth year, before school, before a dawning knowledge of war, before an early loss of place.

On weekends there were welcome diversions: trips in my uncle's Heinz's VW (Freda mostly did not join him). We drove into the pine-fragrant mountains that rose above the town, visited overgrown castle ruins from the seventeenth century and walked through vineyards with vistas into valleys where acres of fruit trees flourished in the warm sunshine, giving the area the name, "Germany's breadbasket," officially known as *Kaiserstuhl* or Emperor's Chair.

Weekdays, I wandered through the narrow cobblestone streets of our quaint town where mountain water ran in neatly contained rivulets along the curbs, the town's ingenuous sanitation system, which didn't even seem remotely necessary: no one ever tossed anything into the street that belonged in a trash can. Nor did they throw garbage into the rushing, clear curbside streams. Even though I was poised to criticize everything about my new home, I could not possibly find fault with the pristine beauty and carefully reconstructed ancient buildings that the war had destroyed.

At the center of town, in a lovely square of cobblestones worn smooth by centuries of pedestrian traffic, soared the Freiburg *Muenster* or cathedral, a marvel of gothic elegance built with the soft red stone of the region. In the afternoon light, its warm glow enveloped the surrounding marketplace in shades of deep rose that pierced the lengthening shadows as the farmers gathered up their unsold wares and loaded them onto simple wooden wagons. They would return the next morning with their colorful cornucopia of strawberries, apples, tomatoes, lettuce, peaches, potatoes, baked goods, cheeses, sausages and on and on. It was hard to imagine in 1957 that there had been a war and a lean aftermath as I walked across that cathedral square and breathed in the fragrances of the perfectly displayed goods and heard the clink of coins in the simple metal boxes that served as cash registers.

Still, my relatives could only afford to serve meat twice a week and we all took a full hot bath only every few days to conserve the gas that heated our water and fueled the old, black kitchen stove. My grandmother presided over the kitchen and saw to it that my teenage cousin, Claus, his mother and I all had one warm meal in the middle of every day.

Nanette was divorced before the war ended. She had been married to a filmmaker in Hamburg who was recruited as a pilot early in the war. He survived countless missions and conquered his fear with the help of mind-altering drugs that were routinely administered to pilots before each mission and that left many broken and addicted if they managed to return home alive. She never spoke of her marriage except to say that the war had made her married life untenable. Instead she turned all her energies towards forging a new, stable life for herself and her son. Never once did I hear her criticize her husband. Upholding his image as a brave, good man was one of the many gifts she gave to Claus who revered his father and longed always to be with him as one longs so often for what is sadly out of reach.

Slowly my eyes opened to struggles far greater than mine. Often the talk at mealtime was about the war. "How did you come to Freiburg from Hamburg?" I asked Nanette after I had thawed enough to turn my attention to others.

"Your grandmother settled here when she left Berlin because Freda was here. Heinz is from this part of Germany and moving south and away from industrial sites that were targets for the Allies' bombs was a good idea. Nonetheless, Freiburg's center was leveled during the war. But we got here just after that."

"Where did you live when you first came?" I wondered.

"Claus and I lived with your grandmother in two small rooms just five minutes from here. We had a one-burner hot plate for meals and a sink that doubled as a place to wash oneself. The rooms looked out onto the small stream you walk alongside to go to school. The view was very pretty and peaceful and we looked into a small group of shade trees by the stream. It was an old house with cracks in the walls from the tremor of bombs," she trailed off, brushing back a strand of hair in a weary gesture. I didn't ask any more questions that day, guessing that she wished not to recall those early days. But I was to learn more over the months from family conversations. The war was beginning to seep into my life and I was eager to learn more.

Claus was just a baby when they arrived in Freiburg and Nanette needed work and a police permit to live there, a requirement that was universal in Germany. Uncle Heinz, ever kind and compassionate, arranged for her living permit, using a cunning that was quite foreign to his straight-laced, law-abiding nature. It was best not to ask for details, I surmised. She soon found work (not possible till one had procured a residency permit) with a medical association of doctors where she began as a secretary working long days. She took a trolley home for lunch daily to be with Claus, then returned to work till nearly seven. That routine was maintained throughout my time in Freiburg.

Grandmother, whom we all called Amma, prepared all meals and supervised Claus's homework. No one supervised mine, a refreshing surprise for one who had experienced entirely too much supervision. Here I was treated as an adult and expected to behave like one. But that was leisurely in coming.

I rarely lingered after meals, retreating to my small room, which was one of four such mansard rooms. A heavy, dusty maroon curtain separated these rooms from a drafty stairwell of worn stone steps that led to the apartments below.

School was always over around 12:30 so afternoons were a time I used more often for trips into town on a borrowed bike than to do homework. I was interested only in German class, which consisted of studying German literature and perfecting one's writing skills. The latter was achieved by assigned topics, which we were to expound upon in an *Aufsatz* or essay that tested our reasoning as much as the clarity of our writing style. Often themes were lofty, philosophical and based on something we had read in class.

Had I shown as much interest in my other subjects, I might have flourished at the *Droste Huelshoff School* but I was stubbornly resistant to Latin, Mathematics and Biology and my grades reflected it. Of course I excelled in English, though I was bored with the grammar and resentful of the comments about my American accent. English was taught with a British accent thought to be far superior and more elegant. Still, there was a palpable admiration for Americans and their goods, which were still fresh memories from the war—from liberation. Coca-Cola was not readily available in stores at that time but many knew it from military rations the American soldiers often shared with hungry Germans.

Once again, I was an oddity. My classmates saw me as an Americanized *Adelige* or member of the aristocracy as attested to by the *von* in my name. I would have much preferred having had a common name and blending more readily into my new world.

I was different, foreign and hard to accept by my peers, although I was given credit for not pushing my family background. It would never have occurred to me to do so as I saw my parents and their elitist values as just short of heinous.

It did not help that Amma, though a commoner by birth and marriage, aspired to the nobility as only those who stand just outside that circle often do. She certainly needn't have done so as she came from a prominence that far surpassed that of Father's family. She was a cousin of Walter Gropius, the ground-breaking architect of the Bauhaus School, and carried that name till she married my partly Jewish grandfather, John Menger.

Her fascination with the aristocracy was evident in her faithful reading of the *Adelsblatt*, a quarterly, if I recall correctly, that gave news of individuals and families of noble birth. It reported on balls attended exclusively by the nobility, marriages, births, deaths, achievements and occasionally even travails. Nearly everything was newsworthy if the "newsmaker" had a title or at least a *von* in their name.

She promptly launched a campaign for me to attend such balls and gatherings. It failed miserably and I managed to avoid even one single such event. While Amma was deeply disappointed in me she remained ever the diplomat and strategist, abandoning all further efforts. Undoubtedly she attributed her failure to my "total Americanization". For, had I not been sent to Germany to reverse that very mark of my character? She must have felt that it was too late to rescue her over-democratized granddaughter.

"I understand your sentiment," she said with conviction after one of our heated discussions about an upcoming party I refused to attend. "After all, you have spent many years in America where no on knows of these old families and the traditions they have passed down. These traditions gave us something to hold on to even while the war challenged us with so many indignities—with hunger, loss and hardship. You have been fortunate not to have known these things," she added, wise enough not to elaborate further on my good fortune.

What were those life-supporting traditions, I wondered? How could beliefs, manners and customs of the privileged help anyone through hardship except to give them an illusion of entitlement? Perhaps visualizing a state of being is half the train ticket to one's destination, I mused.

Amma was a complex woman, one who also possessed a keen sense of justice and a kind heart that wished a good life for everyone, no matter what their heritage. She believed equally that democracy was a many faceted ideal and that in reality, we were *not* all created equally.

In the world of Kaiser Wilhelm, her world, *noblesse oblige* reigned. The nobility's genteel lifestyle and principles were destined, she felt, as a beacon for those unfortunate enough to live in the half-shadows as commoners. In a deft flight of fancy, she never counted herself among those in the shadows. But she always kept up her side of the bargain by living an exemplary life. Amma gave of herself generously.

She chose to buy wilted vegetables and shriveled potatoes from a needy woman who lived off her small plot of land on the outskirts of town and delivered her modest goods by motorcycle in small quantities. When we complained about the moldy potatoes, Amma reminded us that Maidy, as she was nicknamed, surely went to bed hungry on many a night.

Amma also donated whatever goods she could spare to the meager household of a woman who helped occasionally with cooking and cleaning and employed her as much for the housekeeper's needs as for her own. In fact, household help was a distinct luxury for Amma and Nanette.

While not a regular churchgoer, she set aside time every day to converse with God though she never prescribe any spiritual practices for others nor chided us for not attending church except on high holidays.

Amma was never too tired, despite a weak heart, to spend hours with her grandchildren's homework, or make dozens of jellies every August to last us throughout the winter. For days she sat tirelessly at the kitchen table, cooked, pureed and canned.

And unfailingly, she gave love and support to all of us no matter how much she might have disapproved of our behavior. I certainly had become a prime recipient of her generosity and she showed me that I needn't agree with every belief she held to have a general respect and admiration for her.

It was not long before I began to coax family stories out of Nanette. My favorite one about Amma dates back to late in the war. Amma lived in a five-story apartment building in Berlin, together with Nanette and my uncle Christer, Nanette's older brother. The British were lobbing over phosphorous bombs, which, on impact, would burn continuously and could not be extinguished by water or suffocation.

One such bomb crashed into the stairwell right by her entrance and smoldered there on a stone step. Amma reviewed the situation and decided that its heat would serve well as a cooking fire, for which there was neither sufficient wood nor coal in wartime; electric stoves did not exist.

Nanette recalls seeing her mother resolutely add a few pieces of shattered wood banister to the fire and then haul out a large iron pot of water, throw in some potato peels, a few carrots and turnips and a bit of lard, all that was available, and proceed to prepare soup for all the residents of the building.

"She never spoke of the bomb but she did mention that the soup was the first warm meal all of them had enjoyed in days," Nanette reported.

For my second summer in Germany, Nanette arranged for me to spend seven weeks in France near Orleans to help me catch up to my classmates in French. There I pedaled ten kilometers daily to the tiny village that was the nearest marketplace to *Chateau Chaussepôt* where I lived with a family that had somehow missed entry into the twentieth century.

Aside from French lessons every morning, I occupied myself with tedious trips in a row boat on the moat that surrounded the 17th century castle where I lived with two elderly aunts, the husband of one and their mildly retarded teenage nephew. The daily challenge, aside from mastering French, was to catch frogs in the moat with my hands and overcome my boredom at harvesting potatoes in the hot late summer sun with the younger of the two aunts. It helped me acquire a somewhat agrarian vocabulary for which I had no later use.

At the end of my stay, I was rewarded with a three-day trip to Paris in the company of the potato-digging aunt. She had a long-time friend there and we stayed at her musty, dimly lit apartment inhabited also by her beloved cat, a monstrously huge, playful beast that shared our dinner table by perching as a centerpiece and begging for morsels.

I loved the eccentricity and originality of the lady and was more than happy to endure the hard day bed onto which I sank exhausted after many hours of sightseeing. At the end of each day we celebrated with several glasses of fine but simple *vin ordinaire* that whetted our appetites for the delicious meal that awaited us. In that summer, I gained ten pounds and not since have I eaten such crisp, thinly sliced *pommes frîtes* nor had *crème caramel* that even approached what I enjoyed in those weeks of extravagant culinary delights in France. A shocking photo of me attests to the indulgences of that summer. I had fat cheeks and an expanded bosom above a thickened waist.

Not long after I returned, I was paid a visit by a very charming man whom I had met earlier through my parents in New York. He was from an old noble family and had been sent over from Germany to apprentice with a major American bank. My father would not have paid much attention to him had it not been for his family name, which assured him a dinner invitation to our house in Riverdale.

In spite of myself, I liked his easy, unpretentious manner and genuine curiosity about America. His family lived in an ancient castle in the vicinity of Kassel, which had been in the family for hundreds of years. I would not have known anything about his home had Father not queried him at length about his lineage and the family's lands. I was deeply embarrassed by Father's obvious delight in Siegfried's heritage and equally impressed by the offhanded yet courteous manner in which Siegfried responded.

He was a handsome man, tall with sandy-colored hair and very intense blue eyes that wandered my way more often than I would have expected. I remember his smile of encouragement when I nearly spilled the coffee I handed to him with uncertain hands. "Thank you so much. You needn't have served me," he said. "The coffee service is right within my reach." No sense of entitlement there.

A week later he called and asked my mother if he might invite me out to dinner. In his world, that was the proper channel to me and my parents predictably found his traditional manners impressive. After consulting with Father, they both decided that a date was not just permissible but welcome from their vantage point. If there was a small blight on the event, it was merely due to the sanction of my parents. I sniffed the air and determined that marriage hopes were on their minds, a thought that was in general concept downright odious to me. Why on earth would I want to imprison myself in a contract that could play out like that of my parents, nice as Siegfried was?

I saw myself entombed in a drafty German castle with nothing to do all day but roam the woods and perhaps feed the animals; there had to be horses, cows, sheep dogs and sundry other beasts, I reasoned. But my next thought was that I'd be resented by the farm hands that were undoubtedly present in vast numbers and would seek to defend their turf. I was way ahead of myself, of course, and caution had become the mother of anxiety.

Still, I managed to put those thoughts aside on the two evenings that Siegfried and I spent together dining in Manhattan. I have no recollection of the place or the cuisine, much less its location. I do recall that I found him charming, maddeningly polite and foreign in a subtly intriguing way. There was a sweet solicitousness about him and an engaging curiosity about my life as a German girl in America.

"Would you like to visit Germany and learn more about your roots?," he asked me on our second and final date for I was returning to complete my senior year of high school in Maine. I articulated a lukewarm interest, all the while sensing the outer edges of my gently budding interest in a world beyond my own.

So on that fine spring day in 1958, Siegfried, having announced with a phone call his visit to Freiburg in conjunction with a business trip to the area, arrived in the *Loretto Strasse* where I lived and paid my grandmother and me a call. He made a deep bow over her hand and kissed it, thanking her for receiving him on such relatively short notice. Then he turned to me and gave me a radiant smile, taking both my hands in his and with a faint blush to his cheeks, said simply that he was glad to see me again, this time on the European continent. I was not sure what he was really glad about: seeing me or seeing me on German soil. Either way, he seemed pleased and I banished my uncertainty and decided to see where the meeting would take us.

I remember an awkward hour having tea in the living room that doubled as Nanette's bedroom and being somewhat at a loss for words as my grandmother directed tactful questions to Siegfried about his family, their home and his previous stay in New York. Still, it was a thinly disguised probe into his eligibility as a suitor for me with a sharp focus on his family history.

"Of course, I know of your family, which has been in the Kassel area for nearly 700 years. It is so important to have roots, is it not—to relate to a region and know that you will always belong there." Now the voice of displacement, of having been thoroughly dislocated, was speaking with longing and sadness and I felt my grandmother's nostalgia for her *Osterode* home in the East Prussia of another time.

"Yes, we are most fortunate, having been located in the west of Germany. I love the old ramparts of our home and the history they represent. It is not easy to keep up the lands but my parents are determined that they remain in the family. There is considerable forest land that requires tending at great cost" he trailed off.

And so it went: Formal, polite, deferential to my grandmother who sat in regal, quiet dignity, her hands folded in her lap of soft pale silk—her best dress and one of only two outfits that were always perfectly laundered.

Another two weeks passed and I received a call from Siegfried inviting me for a weekend at the home of his parents at *Schloss (*Castle*) Canstein* in the province *of Nordrhein Westfalen.* I cannot say that I was elated about the prospective visit but I was certainly curious and saw it as an opportunity to have a new life experience: a glance into a very old world I did not know first hand. I wanted to know what it feels like to reside within ancient walls, walk through forests of century old trees and experience chivalry on the cusp of its demise.

I took a train to *Kassel*, changing there for a short ride to the village of *Marsberg* near *Heddinghausen*, an equally small hamlet tucked in between rolling hills, meadows and well-tended groves of old trees. I have yet to see an unruly, neglected forest in Germany.

Siegfried met my train and greeted me with a warm smile, then kissed my hand and reached for my small suitcase. "I am so happy to see you and be able to show you my home. I think it will be quite a contrast to America," he added without a trace of innuendo. He was merely stating a fact that was soon to be born out.

We climbed into his car and started down small country roads lined with poplars. Cows grazed in small patches of meadow dotted with yellow wildflowers. It was early summer and the sun cast golden medallions of light between the trees creating playful contrasts that seemed to dance before our eyes as we headed towards *Schloss Canstein.*

The castle announced itself rather suddenly as we came out of a small bend in the road and started down a modest promenade of old trees that led to the compact, stately yet simple structure that towered over a small courtyard. The far end of the building had a sturdy tower that was to be my room for the night.

As we disembarked, a butler came to greet us and to welcome me, then attending immediately to my luggage before I could even reach for it in the trunk of Siegfried's car. I felt a bit peculiar and helpless for the first time in my life. What was one allowed to do on one's own here, I wondered. In fact, was there anything to do here at all or was this merely the way newcomers were treated?

The answer was unclear as I observed the polite, solicitous manner in which the elderly butler spoke with Siegfried and expressed his hope that the roads had not been too busy between here and the train station. "There was a nasty collision with a farmer's tractor on that stretch the other day," he noted with a furrowing of his brow.

"So I heard. But it is generally a very quiet corner in which we live," Siegfried said turning to me as though I needed reassurance. I liked his protectiveness, so unfamiliar to me in a man, so chivalrous. Maybe I needed to rethink my blanket rejection of all Old World manners and attitudes, I thought fleetingly.

What remains in my memory most vividly of the weekend was dinner on Saturday evening. In the late afternoon I had retreated to my quarters, a narrow, cozy tower room with sweeping views of fields and forest lands beyond. There were traditional hunting scenes on the walls and a lovely silk, soft-hued cover on the bed.

I changed into a silk blouse and simple velvet skirt, the only dressy outfit I owned, and stood before the small mirror above an antique dressing table for longer than I might have done on other occasions, trying to calm the persistent flutter in my stomach. I sensed the meal would be formal and that I would be under scrutiny by Siegfried's parents. I had met them only briefly upon arriving, a most reserved and stiffly correct exchange of niceties.

The butler's knock on my door announced dinner and I descended to a spacious dining room with generous windows onto gardens that lay serenely in the early evening light. Silver bowls and plates steaming with simple but fragrant dishes graced the table and we all stood behind our chairs until Siegfried kissed his mother's hand, arranged her chair for seating and then positioned me in my tall-backed chair with gentle and quiet certitude. He addressed his parents with the formal "*Sie*" rather than "*Du*," which I found mightily antiquated and stilted. I was now in a world that preceded, by at least half a century, the late 1950s in which we lived. How quaint, how traditional, how retrograde and how poignant was this family's attempt to hold fast to a vanishing world, I thought, as I lifted my knife and fork ever so gingerly.

Fortunately, Siegfried's parents were not interested enough in me to grill me with questions about my life and reason for now living in Germany. Perhaps I am doing them an injustice and they were not asking because they saw my tension and wariness at this ancient roundtable repast. I will never know although the eventual demise of my friendship with their son would indicate that they did not see me as a potential wife for him. There was never a doubt in my mind that he deferred to their judgment in such matters.

The meal passed in a mercifully reasonable time span with conversational spurts that were not unlike a dull and halting recitative in an opera devoid of surprises. I only recall the *rhythm* of talk, not its content. We were attentively served by yet another elderly butler who was quick to meet every need we expressed even when it was as subtly indicated as one's glance at a half empty glass of wine.

After a walk through the forestland of the property the next day, Siegfried, ever attentive to me on our stroll, drove me to the train and I returned to Freiburg early on Sunday evening. I had seen little of his parents that day.

For days I pondered the visit and the time-warped, ancient life that was lived at *Canstein*. I wondered how many other families lived that way in Europe, safely ensconced in their historical walls, in their medieval towers, in their traditional ways. What had the war taught them? How had it changed their thinking, if at all? I simply could not know.

Several more weeks passed and Siegfried announced yet another visit to Freiburg. He was distracted and slightly uncomfortable as we drove up one of the old Black

Forest routes to a higher elevation with wide, serene views over alpine meadows and distant pine forests.

It was there that he took my hands in both of his and told me in a halting voice that he could not marry me for I was Protestant: baffling to me but very real in his Catholic world.

Marry me? While I had sensed that marriage was possibly on his mind in a general way and that he might have vaguely thought of me as a candidate given the invitation to his family home, the imminence of such a commitment was a great surprise to me.

I felt a vague, nagging sadness, not so much for having been rejected as for the loss of someone I had come to see as a protective, loving friend. I felt sadness as well for his deference to parental edicts, to the power that tradition still held over his heart.

Silently I wished independence and fulfillment for him without uttering the words for they would have betrayed the concern I had for his future happiness. But not for one moment did I doubt that it would never have been with me. Far more than religion separated us and I think we both knew it.

Siegfried slipped from my life that day until many months later when he wrote that he had become engaged to a Dutch woman who was Catholic, a rarity in itself. Harmony of sorts had been maintained in a family that had sought homogeneity for seven hundred years.

It was not long after that I began to have many in a series of dreams about being outside a longed for circle and about failing to meet the requirements to pass any number of tests. I sat paralyzed before exam questions I could not begin to answer, stood before doors that shut right before I reached them, was openly disliked by teachers while I watched in considerable pain how other students were favored and respected. I longed to be liked and was always outside the favored inner circle.

Sleep became the enemy, the shadow in which I was invisible to those for whom I most wanted to be brilliantly present. I fought my bitterest battles at night and the more painful they were, the less I sought sleep: a prescription for insomnia.

The abbreviated friendship with Siegfried was certainly not the sole driving force for those dreams but rather a milestone and culmination of at least a decade of seeking to fit in and be accepted. I was a jagged, errant stone trying hard to fit into an established mosaic—trying to become a part of a larger whole, trying to lose my separateness yet seeking my individuality—wondering who I was to become when I finally found my center.

I suspect I might have begun to find my center the day I looked outside myself. It happened on the way to the bathroom.

Meeting Lars was inevitable and our first encounter was memorably awkward as we nearly collided in the dark hallway on the way to the lone toilet that four of us tenants shared. Our hands brushed as we reached for the light switch in the hall and Lars stepped aside, startled and embarrassed, letting me enter first. I remember the heat that flooded my face as I ducked into the small concrete clad toilet with its high, cobwebbed window.

He was a student who was two years older than I and vastly more advanced than his years. Lars had a passionate and keen interest in literature, ideas and jazz. At nineteen, he was publishing short, pithy parables in the *Berliner Morgenpost*. I doubt the editor was aware of his age nor was it relevant other than to mark his exceptionality. He received a modest fee of ten Deutsch Marks per published piece and it was very real money to him in those days for he was a refugee from Poland.

His father had been murdered by the Poles at the end of the war[1], his two sisters and brother scattered amongst relatives in the West. Lars lived in a tiny room across from mine and ate meals with my aunt Freda's family, which knew his mother.

I was to learn in time that his mother had been imprisoned by the Poles at the end of the war as a German national and, upon her release after five bitter years of abuse, had found work in a Black Forest sanatorium. She was unable to care for her four children who were scattered around Germany and London, surviving largely by their own ingenuity.

His was a solitary childhood whose early years were spent in a small village in the mountains of the Black Forest at a remote, austere boarding school until he came to live in the mansard across from mine as a teenager. Though Lars never spoke of, much less complained about, the years of deprivation right after the war, I learned later from others that he was often hungry. But so were millions of other Germans, probably making it feel inappropriate to speak of a hardship that knew no uniqueness.

---

1.   The family lived in northwestern Poland, which was variously occupied by Germans over the centuries. Lars's father was slain as a "Nazi sympathizer," a verdict readily applied to German Poles after 1944 if they had not resisted Hitler.

Ours was a bittersweet romance and we stumbled awkwardly through the bewildering emotions and insecurities that beset us. I was wild and adventurous, ready to explore everything I did not yet know. He was tender and painfully introverted. We read poetry, listened to music and told of our lives and of our fears.

But when he held me in the night on my narrow, hard cot, I never had bad dreams. We learned to turn gently and fold our bodies into one another, careful not to awaken the other. In the tender innocence of children, we believed in love and we trusted one another. That is, until I abused that trust, not understanding that we wandered in a rare and precious garden.

I must have believed that nothing would change in our perfect union the rainy afternoon Lars was away and I tumbled into our bed with a near stranger who told me I was beautiful.

When Lars learned from a friend of my betrayal, he turned to stone. And everything between us changed forever He could not forgive me and I was unable to forgive myself. The law of Karma had revealed itself and it was harsh. For well over two years I sought to gain his forgiveness and regain his love but the wound I had inflicted was mortal. I was nearly twenty and more alone than I had ever been. Worse yet, I was devastated by impotent regret.

The Freiburg years had passed very rapidly and my Green Card was about to expire. I was deeply sad at the prospect of leaving but not prepared to burn my bridges to America by losing my re-entry visa, which was good for just two years, now nearly completed.

It was late spring and the time was fast approaching to leave behind a German life I had come to love: wandering across the cobblestone marketplaces surrounding centuries old churches and cathedrals, marveling at the weathered ancient walls that had defended the small rural towns I visited, and exchanging stories with the family which had forgiven me my early tirades and reached out with love to show me that their ways were worth examining and melding into my American experiences.

As departure loomed I thought of Gina once again. I longed to see her before three thousand miles would once again stretch between us. I calculated that she must be close to eighty and that there was undoubtedly not much time left for meeting.

So I planned a trip to Vienna. It was a dozen years since we had last seen one another and the prospect of seeing Vienna through her eyes was also very compelling.

I took a leisurely train from Freiburg—a glorious trip of 15 hours through breathtaking alpine landscapes canopied by towering cloud formations and shafts of sunlight that melted the last snow in the shadowy hollows. Cows grazed on high meadows strewn with wildflowers; wooden, wind-beaten lean-to huts dotted the mountainsides; shepherds driving their herds waved to us as we whistled through the gorges and alongside the rich pastures; and snowy peaks crowned the verdant hillsides.

I lowered my window and was rewarded with the sound of cowbells and the fragrance of a high-meadow spring. A heady rush of joy swept over me and I thanked the nameless spirit in the sky for the beauty He had bestowed on this peaceful, contented corner of the world. I longed to hold fast the unadulterated magnificence that sped by all too swiftly to the steady thump and roll of our wheels on the tracks. Nothing had changed over the centuries in those Alps and there was a deep comfort in that.

Gina had come to meet my train, she now a mildly stooped figure dressed in a simple black dress that reached nearly to her ankles. Her hair had turned white in the dozen years since I had last seen her but her eyes had not lost any of their luster. Her smile was radiant and vibrant, denying her years and transforming her face into a testimony of joy.

We hugged for a very long time and tears streaked our cheeks when we finally pulled apart to look into one another's eyes. And in that moment, I remembered keenly how much I had missed her, often in the quiet hours of night, over the years that had bridged China and America for me—China and Austria for her.

Gina lived in a second floor walk-up flat of an old, solid building in a part of town dotted with small green squares. Here there were ample benches filled with elderly people who fed the pigeons or sought a comforting conversation with a stranger or acquaintance to break the silence of loneliness. Sadness pervaded the area and coal smoke hung in the dusky spring air. But Gina was a quiet radiant light in the twilight of her settled familiar life, a world that seemed not to have changed in many decades.

So we sat together and fed breadcrumbs to the pigeons that swirled around us in soft clouds of gray and alighted on the armrests of our bench, cooing companionably as Gina and I revisited Chinese early memories.

"You used to love to sing," she offered as she broke into "*Die Forelle*" and transported me back to the upstairs nursery with its blowing voile curtains. "*In einem Baechlein helle…*," she began as I fought back tears and reached for her withered, worn hand. It was she who had given me the priceless gift of a love for music as she led me into song on many nights before bedtime. And as I tucked into the soft blankets and fragrant sheets that always smelled of lavender, I drifted off to melodies of Schubert and Mozart.

The next two nights, my only ones in Vienna, Gina readied me for bed at eight o'clock, much like she had done over the many years in China. She covered me with a blanket far warmer than I needed, tucked it under my chin and hugged me with a wish that my dreams be sweet and untroubled.

Of course, I was wide awake for hours and alert to the sounds outside my window—the wailing of police sirens, the laughter of animated students who had just left the local *Weinstube* after imbibing the fine wines from vineyards that began just at the edge of the city. How I longed to be with them and yet, how sweet it was to re-live the sheltering warmth of my very early years with her in China. I knew once again the preciousness of the gift she had given. And with it came a bonus: my discovery of the sweetness of gratitude. Thank you, dearest Gina, wherever you are today.

Revisiting My First Home, Tsingtao

In the mid-1980s I realized a long-held dream and revisited China as one of a small group of journalists charged with travel story assignments. At the end of the trip, I added on a few days to visit Tsingtao.

I needed to confirm my memories and find a way to dispel the sense of loss—of being cut off forever from tangible evidence of my earliest years. Often in America, I had wondered whether I merely *dreamt* of wooden junks with tattered sails, emaciated men laboring to pull rickshaws through garbage strewn streets, teeming markets swarming with flies and dirty, ragged children with wide, anguished eyes. I wondered also whether I had merely imagined our magical garden with its fragrant arbor of wisteria, the goldfish pond and the peonies that Mother lovingly cut and arranged in a large silver bowl that always announced summer for me.

With the patient help of a young guide, Wei, who spoke remarkably good English and missed no opportunity to riddle me with questions about Michael Jackson, which I was woefully unable to answer, we wandered the streets of Tsingtao in a blazing August sun. Gone were the rivers of sewage flowing in the gutters; gone were the half naked children clad in pants with rear end flaps to facilitate evacuating instantly by the roadside, and rickshaws were more a curiosity than an ubiquitous part of the street scene.

The open market downtown was neat and offered a wide variety of goods from clothing to fresh produce, meats, shoes and fabrics. Old women, their feet no longer bound, carried baskets of rats, normal fare for most urban, well-situated burghers, and food stands offered steaming dumplings, a specialty of the province.

I bought a T-shirt with Chinese lettering that said "Tsingtao". The cotton was of a thin, soft quality that looked cool and absorbent and I relished the thought of changing out of my sweat-soaked denim shirt that drew envious glances from all the young people. It was emblematically American and clearly coveted but I could not think of a way to change in the market and give it away without standing in the midst of a jostling, tittering crowd in my bra.

As we wended our way through the stands, Wei told me that he was a part-time disk jockey at the local radio station and loved all American pop music, placing Madonna right up amidst the Gods of Pop alongside Michael Jackson. His round face brightened at the mention of their names and his hands did an animated mid-air dance, endearing him to me despite my inability to share his passion. I mentioned Count Basie and Duke Ellington, Louis Armstrong and Miles Davis to see if we could expand the scope of our conversation but only drew a blank, slightly uncomfortable stare.

We lunched in Tsingtao's best restaurant, a large, open, busy emporium of fleet-footed waiters bringing us steaming dumpling dishes garnished with crisply cooked cabbage. Wei beamed with delight and we both ate with gusto while perspiration poured from our faces into the food and cups of scalding tea. I was ready for a nap afterwards but we persevered and trudged onward towards the sea to look for the street I had left nearly 40 years earlier. I remembered it as a hilly dirt lane that abutted a seaside boulevard, which separated the town from a narrow stretch of sand dotted with large brown rocks.

But I did not expect there to be a *number* of such streets, now paved and potholed. It took us fully two days to finally arrive at the street that was once called "Rising Sun" but had no street sign, not that I recall it ever did. Mother had said its former name before I left for China.

That night, I stayed in a faceless concrete block of a hotel by the sea. Though my window faced the Yellow Sea, I saw no junks, as in my youth, just fishermen casting their nets into a placid sea that lapped at the shore gently. I longed for crashing waves and sea spray that might have misted the dusky horizon on my first day back in Tsingtao. I was not to be rewarded with any such remnants of my youth on that melancholy evening.

After a dinner of rice and vegetables at the hotel, I wandered down to the water's edge, which was now dotted with small cabanas, and offered a wood plank promenade equipped with a blaring sound system. That evening, Leroy Anderson's "Blue Tango" from the early 1950s played repeatedly, overpowering the soughing of the sea and taunting the slice of moon that cast a silent, silver ribbon across the water.

I walked for hours that night, breathing in the familiar scent of the seaside pines and watching the moon's light cast shifting shadows on the rocks among which I had played as an eight-year old. I felt a profound longing and sadness for what could never be retrieved or even re-lived. Still, I was deeply grateful for the chance to at least return and transform old dreams into vividly remembered realities.

The next day was slightly cooler and I wore my new T-shirt and a pair of worn sandals that allowed my feet to breathe. By ten in the morning, the beach was swarming with bathers of all ages. No one was swimming. There was literally no room. People waded into the murky water and splashed one another, staying behind the ropes that were a warning that sharks were plentiful beyond.

We walked along the beach towards a configuration of large reddish-brown rocks that seemed particularly familiar to me. "The road must go up right from here," I told Wei excitedly.

And then there it was! Unmistakably, our street meandered up the hill past low, simple wooden houses that I did not recognize and yet, it all seemed familiar. I cannot explain the certainty I felt, the sense of finally being home, the rush of joy, the excitement and the tears that began to well behind my lids.

"We are here…this is it, it all comes back to me," I blurted without restraint or reason. Wei was quiet, a bit puzzled but gentle in his responses. "I am so happy—it is good for you, yes?" he said simply. I nodded and picked up the pace despite the oppressive heat, which I merely registered but did not really feel as such. A trickle of perspiration became a tingling reminder of being fully present, fully alive: Not a hardship, not even a discomfort.

I glanced to my right where a hovel of squalid houses had once stood, separated from our home by a high stone garden wall. The wall was still there, covered with a tangle of wild vines but the rickety neighboring buildings, courtyard and simple stable that once sheltered a cow, some chickens and a donkey were gone. In their place was a faceless stone structure that appeared to be home to several families and numerous children playing in a dusty yard.

We hurried alongside the wall till we came to the small stone guard house with its iron-grated window alongside the tall black iron gate that stood open, giving a view of our old, sprawling stucco house with its wide steps to the French doors that opened onto what had been our spacious garden.

I was dizzy with excitement, yet keenly aware of a dull pain in my chest that spoke to me of longing and melancholy for all that would remain forever, after this day, thousands of miles from my adult life. There would be no subsequent return to this house, I felt—to this land, this beloved sea—no future touching, smelling and tasting these early sensations to re-confirm that they had indeed helped shape and inform the woman I had become.

And as we stepped through the gate, I looked instinctively to my right to find the wisteria walkway where Father strolled every evening after returning from the

Consulate. I came later to think of it as his "Cloister Walk," the walking medita-
tion during which he attempted to assemble his turbulent days into a semblance
of normality and reason. Often I would join him there in the dizzying fragrance
of the wisteria blossoms of summer. We held hands and didn't speak, a very special time for me. A bombastic man gone silent is a remarkable and memorable
phenomenon. I like to remember him just as he was in the arbor those many
years ago.

I must have stood in the cool, fragrant wisteria shade for many minutes that day,
for Wei had quietly seated himself on a large rock nearby to leave me time alone
with my memories. I thanked him silently for his sensitivity as I re-emerged into
the bright August light and headed with him towards the large unremarkable
house that stood solidly in a bright square of sunlight. It had survived so much, I
thought, not least of all the Cultural Revolution.

To the right of the wide front steps, I saw a children's sandbox and immediately
recognized it as the goldfish pond it had been in its former life. At least it had
found a good and happy use, I thought, as I recalled the vibrant golden color of
the flitting fish, catching the bright light in their play, which I had watched with
wonder and delight so long ago.

There was no one in sight anywhere on the property and so we hurried over to
the side entrance by the towering acacia tree, from whose blossoms I sucked sweet
nectar as a child, to see if we could gain entry. It was the entrance we had used
most frequently for it opened directly onto the staircase to the upstairs bedrooms
and to the spacious living room on its right with the French doors that faced the
garden. I ran up the stairs, as sure of my bearings as if the year had been 1948. I
was looking for the large, sunny nursery that faced both the garden and a side terrace and I was rewarded with a room that appeared smaller than in my memory
but was unmistakably Manfred's and my play area. The room was filled with at
least 20 desks for small children and simple wooden toys were piled in the corners
near shelves of writing materials and books. Clearly, our old home was now a
school.

To the left of the door was the small bathroom where Gina had bathed us, still
complete with its claw-footed tub and old porcelain washstand that I could only
reach by stepping on a wooden stool as a six-year old. My heart raced and I was
overcome by a stream of memories—pictures long-forgotten of learning to brush
my teeth with a long-handled, harsh, bristly brush; shuddering with cold as I

stepped out of the warm water and into the large towel Gina held open for me. She could dispense comfort as reliably as a down cover on a cold night.

Suddenly I heard hurried steps on the stairs and shrill female voices speaking excitedly with Wei. Time was clearly running out for my explorations so I rushed into the room that had been my parents' bedroom. There was the small terrace overlooking the garden with its perfect view of the wisteria arbor that was a soft haze of lavender in the sunlight that morning. I fixed the view in my mind, knowing I would want to retrieve the memory repeatedly over the coming years.

All too soon, my reverie was cut short by the strident, angry voices of several women.

I heard Wei presumably trying to explain why we were there but it seemed to have no impact on their ire.

We were to leave immediately or they would call the police, a daunting prospect that conjured up images in my mind of incarceration with no access to a lawyer and possibly the confiscation of my passport. I told Wei to apologize for us and explain that we did not realize we were considered to be trespassing. Then I placed my palms together and bowed, trying with gesture to convey gratitude for the chance to revisit.

I felt deep gratitude and the tears that stung my eyes must have conveyed my feelings. They released us reluctantly and asked once again that we leave immediately. There cannot have been much sympathy for a Westerner who had lived on their soil in such a comfortable, spacious house at the start of China's Cultural Revolution.

I closed a chapter on my life that day, looking out towards the sea from my parents' small terrace, having also reached out to touch the wisteria blossoms and gnarled old vines that had survived the years of chaos the land had known. I finally knew I had not imagined that magical garden and it left me profoundly content as we strode out through the gates that would certainly endure for many more decades. So much had not.

And later that day after Wei had gone his way, I was drawn again to the small cove at the end of our street. Its large brown rocks stood as silent sentinels overlooking a quiet sea, empty of junks and now even of fishermen. I reclaimed it even as young people, strolling hand in hand walked on *my* sands and caught the salty breezes, which had cooled my cheeks for at least seven childhood summers.

As I sat by the small pools of water that lapped between the rock fortresses I had designated as my secret sanctuary some forty years ago, I wondered if separation—or exile, if you will, was a prerequisite for treasuring the foundations of our lives. Do we require loss to perceive what is precious?

Afterword

What has this immigrant's life given me? It has certainly prompted me to think about loss, separation and "not fitting in," not being accepted, while reminding me of the many gifts received along a challenging journey. I would like my life and small hardships to **count**—to help me persevere in the deeply held wish to speak out against bigotry and injustice of all kinds. It is why I finally summoned the courage to write this book, a modest but earnest step.

At what point did I morph from an immigrant to an assimilated, true American, I wonder? What was the unmistakable point of transition, the hallmarks of that migration from guest to full-fledged member of the regular roundtable?

That moment was undoubtedly when I first accepted and trusted the friendship that was genuinely extended to me—extended with no thought of where I came from, who my parents were or how I looked.

It is the moment I *believed* my acceptance because it was given with an open, warm heart that was unmistakably genuine. It was when Jeanne folded me into her world in Louisville, it was when I felt safe in opening my life to her. The foundation laid by our friendship gave me the shaky, hopeful confidence that others might also accept me and, in so doing, they would put America within reach. It started small and I suspect I am not alone in that experience. Mine was a two-fold process of acceptance, first by others and then by myself.

It seems self-evident, then, that healthy nationhood calls for tolerance and the extension of humanity to its wanderers, its pilgrims, its refugees before they can kindle patriotism in their hearts and transform from passive and often frightened migrants to productive, rooted citizens. In the late 1940s, we entered such a healthy nation.

Many decades later, on one of my frequent trips to Germany, I was reminded once again how precious and sustaining tolerance is by witnessing, once again, its opposite. It was just a small incident. While visiting an acquaintance, born during the Second World War, she handed me a book by a Jewish author and said, "Here. I think you will like this…as you are such a Jew-lover."

I was too stunned to respond. Also, there would have been no point in commenting as her brand of intolerance was deeply inbred, intractable and the product of living her whole life in a totally homogeneous upper class society that rarely ever met up with Jews, blacks, Muslims, Arabs, or any other ethnic group outside of her own. Hence, her view of "outsiders" was a stereotypical one, handed down over generations and accepted without question or curiosity. Hers is a monochromatic world, brightened but not informed by her extensive travels.

I am reminded of what my husband relates about his very young children, my stepchildren, when they first arrived in Hong Kong where they lived for nearly three years.

So much was new and strange to them and they initially often used the word, "weird" to describe their observations of Asian life and people. "Not weird," he corrected them each time, "just *different*". They absorbed his lesson well and are all without a shred of stereotypical, much less bigoted thinking. I am very proud of them and thankful to him for his lessons. He excited them about differences between people, awakened them to the wonderful kaleidoscopic nature of life, made them enquiring, curious young people with infinite horizons and just hearts.

Today I can say with deep sincerity that I am grateful for the somewhat turbulent and often lonely early life I led. For one, it has made me profoundly grateful for the love, friendship and acceptance I have received over the last four decades. I will always have bad dreams—dreams of exclusion and rejection by peers. But today they are merely very old flickering shadows remaining on the outer surfaces of my subconscious. Not the reality of nightmares they once were.

I have had to think longer than most about what I hold dear, what is worth defending and about the complexities of the human heart, which defy facile judgments. People and issues don't come in neat, clear-cut packages. Father was selfish and unbridled but was often also kind and loving, a blindly patriotic, naïve dreamer but also, finally, a small voice against Hitler. He was perhaps more clay-footed than most but an examination of his early life has helped me find compassion and forgiveness, as has Mother. And with those sentiments come peace and closure.

Finally, I am left with a troubling question as I look back on my family history in the dark Hitler years. Had today's American political climate reigned in 1948, would America have turned us away at its gates or even later deported us as it has done with many innocents of the Muslim faith in the aftermath of 9/11? I will leave you to answer the question for yourself. America was certainly an open-hearted, compassionate land in the late 1940s, albeit less fearful, and I am deeply grateful for the gifts it dared to give my family.

We were woefully square pegs not fitting in to round holes, if you will, and it took years to shed that feeling but it was no different for countless others who arrived on these shores.

I only wish I would have scratched some prescient, encouraging words on the walls of the detention center in San Francisco back in 1948 to give courage to the masses of immigrants who passed through those doors into freedom after us. In hindsight, I might have written:

"Be proud to be unique and different. Wear it well with pride and courage and others will honor your singular radiance."

I know I would have benefited immensely from my own belatedly imagined advice.

978-0-595-38652-9
0-595-38652-0